A Manual for
Woman's Self-Defense

Michael G. V. Pickering

The Athletic Institute
200 Castlewood Drive
North Palm Beach, Florida 33408

Library of Congress Catalog Card Number 82-074558
ISBN 87670-088-1

Published by
THE ATHLETIC INSTITUTE
200 Castlewood Drive
North Palm Beach, FL 33408
U.S.A.

Table of Contents

Foreword

The American public has accepted martial arts as a means of self-defense rather than as a competitive sport or a mental, psychological, religious, or physiological study. Many schools, universities, and YMCAs, for example, have adopted the martial arts into their curriculum in recent years.

The term *self-defense* is so broad that it could be pursued as a major academic discipline. In *A Manual for Woman's Self-Defense*, self-defense has been appreciatively handled by the author as an extension of the martial arts. He distinguishes between the self-defense aspect of martial arts and the sports aspect, which emphasizes the aesthetic and psychological side requiring long, ritual training.

Michael Pickering has taught at the University of California (Berkeley) as a Martial Arts Instructor specializing in the self-defense area. In this book he has described all the important victimology points and has organized and expressed the material in such a way as to benefit everyone, from beginners to experts. He was encouraged to publish this book as a contribution to the field.

I am proud to have written the Foreword to this book and to have been closely associated with the author.

Kyung Ho (Ken) Min

Kyung Ho (Ken) Min *has long been recognized as one of the leaders in martial arts in this country. His name is respected worldwide in the Korean martial arts of Tae Kwon Do and Hapkido, and in the Japanese martial art of judo. He has done much in this country to promote these arts and get them accepted as a part of American culture. He has served as president of the United States Amateur Athletic Union Judo Foundation and the United States Amateur Athletic Union Tae Kwon Do Federation.*

Part 1

Preparation Is The Key

1

Introduction to Self-Defense

A sexual assault occurs in the United States every nine minutes. Until women learn to defend themselves that statistic will remain the same or increase.

There are two ways for women to learn self-defense: in a class or through a book written by an expert. Unfortunately, there are problems with either approach: Most instructors and books are oriented in one direction, i.e., in karate, judo, or whatever other martial art in which the instructor or author is trained. This is fine as far as it goes, but this type of specialized emphasis is not necessarily effective in a real street situation. If an attacker does not move in an orthodox or familiar pattern, it is easy for the defender to become confused.

This book maintains that one type of training is not enough. The woman interested in learning how to defend herself should know several methods that she *can use automatically in real street or home situations.*

The few self-defense books that do try to cover more than one type of training (karate, judo, jiu-jitsu or other combinations of martial arts techniques) either try to cover too much or don't give enough practical information. Some state "Do such-and-such when this happens, and such-and-such when that happens." Unfortunately, there is no way to cover every single possible situation and any book or course that makes this claim is pretty much a waste of time and money. Other books espouse techniques that take years and years of practice to master. And still others teach methods that are downright stupid and dangerous, that this author (who has black belts in tae kwon do and hapkido, a brown belt in judo, plus several other belts in other martial arts, and over twelve years experience in self-defense teaching) wouldn't try under any circumstances.

Inside *A Manual For Woman's Self-Defense,* you will learn

aspects of self-defense rarely taught in classes and books.

- Getting out of grabs, and avoiding grabs and strikes
- Protecting yourself with techniques that are simple and require very little strength—even if the attacker is much larger than yourself
- A basic method of moving that with some practice is as easy as walking
- Counter techniques
- Blocking techniques
- The physical, mental, and legal aspects of self-defense
- Nonphysical or nonviolent ways of getting out of life-threatening situations, a subject ignored in almost all self-defense books
- Using weapons, and whether or not you should use them, how to use them, and how to defend against them

The book is written in such a manner that readers can teach themselves and practice what is offered. It can also be used for teachers of self-defense as a full course outline or as a supplement to their courses. The book is oriented toward the female student, but males will also find the techniques in here practical and useful. The techniques are designed for the weaker person; most attacks are going to be initiated by a bigger and stronger person, so it is necessary to learn things that anyone can do regardless of size.

2
Prepare Yourself

Every physical activity demands at least some strength and endurance, and the art of self-defense is no different. There are basically four areas to be concerned with: arm strength, leg strength, abdominal strength, and endurance. Each will be discussed in turn.

Arm Strength

A certain amount of arm strength is necessary for blocking, releasing (from grabs), and striking. If you hit an attacker in self-defense you will want it to hurt; you don't want the attacker to start laughing at the ineffectiveness of the punch or strike. Some people have "iron" stomachs or jaws, and an ineffective punch isn't going to do much good. How does one build up arm and elbow striking strength? One way is through exercise: pushups, or weights if they are available. This book concentrates only on exercises that do not require equipment or large amount of space.

Pushups. You must do proper pushups to gain the maximum benefits. Keep the back straight, knees off of the ground, lower the whole body to the ground and push up. Repeat ten times every day. If you can't do ten, then build up to it. If you can't do one, get the ready position and hold, then go down just a little bit and back up each time. Gradually increase the amount of dip. This exercise is great for arm strength, and as a side benefit it helps shoulder, back and abdominal strength. For those who find ten pushups easy, do them on fingertips or fists.

Leg Strength

Leg strength is important for kicking and jumping. Women

can usually hold their own with males in leg strength. There is not much difference between the average woman's and the average man's leg strength (as measured by a percentage of body weight), although in arm strength males still hold a pretty big advantage. To build leg strength all you need to do is climb stairs or do simple squats to chair-seat level (fig. 1,2).

Figure 1

Figure 2

Abdominal Strength

Abdominal strength is very important. Because it is one of the major muscle groups of the body, it helps posture, keeps the stomach from sagging, and helps blood circulation. A strong abdomen can take a fairly strong punch or kick and not be hurt by it. Professional boxers for example, are hit hundreds of times in the abdomen and hardly even feel it. Hopefully, you won't get hit there hundreds of times, but the abdominal muscles should be strong enough to repel at least a moderate punch or kick. The best exercise for the abdominal group is the situp. Do situps with bent knees, and keep the arms folded across the chest. Leg lifts are also good; keep the head off the floor and look at the feet. These exercises take care of the upper and lower abdominals. Add some twisting to the situps and that will get the side muscles also.

Endurance

To increase endurance, alternate jogging with some bursts of fairly fast running. If you are attacked, you don't want to be exhausted after ten to twenty seconds—you might have to fight for four or five minutes or longer. Don't rely on extra adrenaline to carry you through; ninety-nine percent of the time it isn't going to help.

If the chance to run occurs take it! You don't want to be exhausted and collapse after fifty yards. If someone is chasing you, you might have to run a fairly long way for help or to get away.

Before starting any of these exercises or taking a self-defense class take a physical exam from your doctor, especially if you are middle-aged or haven't done any exercising in a long time. Do the exercises until you are tired; don't overexert yourself.

These exercises are fairly simple, easy to do, and necessary. They will help you to be prepared for any self-defense situation. Statistics from the University of California (Berkeley) Rape Prevention Program have shown that an attacker, especially a rapist, tends to pick out shy, frail women. If you exercise, you are going to feel better, your step will be a little quicker, you will be more sure of yourself and possibly eliminate an attack because of your appearance. So get started now!

MENTAL ASPECTS

Mental aspects consist mainly of keeping cool in any type of situation. Of course, this is easier said than done, but it is possible. One way to keep cool is to continually practice the movements and techniques so that if an attack does occur you react automatically, even if surprised, and respond even before you have time to "lose your cool" or become afraid. This will take dedicated training—not once or twice a year. Two to three minutes of repetition every day or every other day is much better than no training or sporadic training. You will be surprised at the results.

Another way to react calmly is to go over various self-defense situations in your mind. Go over them several times all the way from the beginning to the end. Project an image of the attacker, how he will attack, your response, and the ending. It is important to get a mental image of the self-defense situation and important to carry the projection all the way to the end. This is much harder to do than it sounds. Most people only get about one-half to three-quarters of the way through the projection and then stop. Whether the ending is just getting away, getting hurt, or stopping the attacker cold, it is important to do this exercise, so that if the situation does occur it will be just a rehearsal for you and you will not be panic stricken by the situation.

Another thing to be considered is pain. In any type of physical confrontation the person attacked is going to be hurt. Whether one resists or not, there is going to be some physical pain and more than likely some mental pain in the confrontation. By recognizing and preparing for this inevitability, the pain will be lessened. Remember, you are doing situps and pushups to build up your body strength, so that you can withstand pain if it occurs.

Perhaps the most difficult aspect of any self-defense class is to evoke an aggressive response in the person attacked. If you do decide to resist physically, this is of the utmost importance. Statistics from the Rape Prevention Program indicate that physical resistance is beneficial in stopping an attack about seventy-five to eighty percent of the time. Of those who did successfully resist, over seventy percent had some type of self-defense or martial art class. But violence is a two-sided coin, and the other side is that resistance tends to create a more violent confrontation. The worst thing one can do is to put up a half-hearted resistance. This doesn't offer any real protection for the defender and makes the attackers more violent. So whatever you decide to do, do not do it halfway—either no physical resistance or total all-out resistance.

There is still the problem of overcoming the fear of hurting someone. Most men don't have this problem. Most have been conditioned to the idea of receiving and inflicting pain.

Women, on the other hand, are conditioned to be nice to everyone, to be nonaggressive, meek, and obedient. So when a woman is confronted in a self-defense situation, her training is not to resist, but rather to do as she is told no matter what the consequences. Fortunately, this is changing somewhat as the women's liberation movement continues. More women are becoming involved in sports and business competition and making more decisions regarding their own lives.

Some hard questions are raised in chapter 15 regarding a newly identified type of rape. Aquaintance rape has always been a problem, but not identified as rape in the past. There is a very thin line in some cases between seduction and forcible seduction. Some ideas on how the woman can take charge of the situation through communication will be discussed.

Whose fault is it anyhow? Many women blame themselves for a rape and many men blame women for enticing rapes, and then for not resisting enough if a rape does occur. It is bad enough if a woman is physically raped. But, to face all of this extra pressure from herself, her friends, her family, the police, hospital staffs, judges, etc., etc., makes the situation unbearable to many. To avoid this guilt situation, especially the self guilt, requires a strong mind and the help of friends and family. It is very important to discuss "what would happen if" a woman is raped.

NONPHYSICAL RESISTANCE

There are other methods that you can use in self-defense situations besides trying to resist physically.

- *Talk.* This will sometimes allow a defender to stall for time until help arrives or the attacker leaves.
- *Do something entirely out of place or unexpected.* You might pretend that the attacker is really cute and so disorient him that he leaves or lets his guard down somewhat.
- *Deceive him.* Shout for some (nonexistent) friend of yours in the next room. You might also do something totally disgusting, such as vomiting on him, or act crazy and start slobbering at the mouth.

There is detailed discussion of these methods in chapter 13.

Remember that you should always be ready for a physical response. There is no guarantee that if you use any of these methods, the attack will stop. There is a point when talking or other things might do no good. You have to be aware of this and be ready to react to the threat.

WEAPONS

Any type of weapon immediately changes a self-defense situation into a life-and-death situation. In this situation you must be totally prepared for anything, and if you decide to resist there must be no hesitation on your part, because it could be fatal. The techniques used in these situations are more deadly and are designed to end a confrontation immediately.

There are also times when you will not be able to do anything. If an attacker has a gun and is several steps away, there isn't much you can do unless he or she gets closer.

One important thing to remember is that if the attacker carries a weapon, he or she cannot be relied on to act logically. To do exactly as one is told does not guarantee survival. The eight Chicago nurses who did exactly what they were told to do, and put up no physical resistance at all, did not live to tell anyone about it.

3

Movement

Movement in a self-defense situation means moving in such a manner as to avoid the attack or at least the major force of the attack. Lack of movement leads to absorbing the full force of the attack and this is not wise. Movement alone does not always guarantee that you will avoid the attack. For example, the defender might move the wrong way, into the force of the attack. Or the attacker might change quickly to adjust to the new direction, in which case the defender will have to keep moving or change direction again. Again, movement alone is often not enough—blocking and countering are also necessary to end the attack. However, movement is the first step.

Before getting into the basics, it is important to understand that it will be necessary for you to practice these things—even if only for a few minutes every day or every other day. You will not need a partner (although it will help), but constant repetition of all the aspects of the book, both physical and nonphysical, are necessary to get full benefits. You will be surprised how much of a difference even three minutes a day will make.

STANCES

Basically, you want a comfortable, well balanced, quick, and easily achieved stance, one from which a person can move in several different directions with either foot, from which is offered the least area of exposure, and which can be easily changed from defensive to offensive.

Figure 3 shows how most people stand—in other words, a normal stance. This stance exposes just about every vulnerable area of the body. The only protected part of the body is the back. Modifications are necessary to protect oneself better.

Figure 3

Figures 4 and 5 show front and side views of the basic defense position, or *natural stance*. The position of the hands protects the side and the front of the body. By moving the hands slightly up or down, the head and lower parts are protected. The legs are fairly close together for rapid movement and for the balance necessary to kick with either leg.

Notice the arm position. The front arm is protecting the rib cage. Make sure the fingertips or the top of the fist are no higher than the chin. The elbow should be a few inches from the body, the arms should be bent approximately ninety degrees at the elbow, and the whole arm should be almost straight up and down. The back arm should be protecting the

Figure 4   Figure 5

front of the body and about halfway between the chest and navel.

There will be more discussion of blocking and arm position in chapter 4. This is the basic defense posture. One should always try to get in this position as quickly as possible. It does not matter which leg is forward; both positions should be practiced. From a normal position the easiest way to get into the posture is to bring one leg directly behind the other leg while moving the hands to the proper position (diags. **1A-1B**).

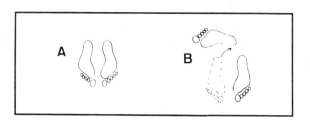

Diagrams 1A —1B

Some stances to avoid are shown in the following figures. Figure 6 shows a karate front stance, usually used when delivering a punch. This stance exposes the groin region and the front knee. Figure 7 leaves the front knee exposed and it is hard to move frontwards or backwards out of this stance. Figure 8 is a judo or wrestlers stance, once again exposing the groin. Although it is easy to grab a groin kick from this stance, it is not easy to grab a full power kick, nor is it easy to block a fake kick with a simultaneous hand technique to the face. There are several other esoteric stances that can be eliminated without further consideration due to their impracticality or the fact that it takes several years to practice to get into them correctly.

Figure 6

Figure 7

Figure 8

DIRECTION OF MOVEMENT

There are thousands of different directions to move, of course, but this chapter is concerned with the four basic directions: forwards, backwards, and sideways (both sides). All the other directions derive from these basic patterns.

The following photos show simple one-step and two-step forward and backward movement. When moving forward, bring the back leg up in front of the front leg (fig. 9). If moving back, do just the opposite, move the front leg behind the back leg (fig. 10). Do not raise the feet high off of the ground unless kicking while moving (diags. 2A-2D).

In two-step forward movement, move first with the front

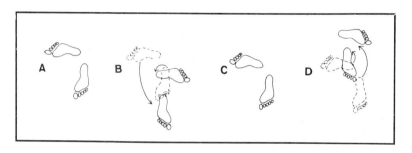

Diagrams 2A — 2B

foot (fig. 11) and bring the back foot up (fig. 12) almost like a sliding motion. This movement pattern can also be used going to the side, just step sideways with the front foot and let the back foot follow. Do not take too big a step, otherwise balance is lost. When moving back, the back foot moves first, then the front foot follows (diags. 3A-3D).

Movement to the side is very important, because it is the easiest way to evade a strike. You can move anywhere between 5 and 180 degrees. Forty-five- and ninety-degree pivots will be emphasized the most as they give the best movement away from the attacker and are the safest. More or less angle creates more risk factors. A good principle to remember is: *Never turn your back to the attacker.* Looking at figure 13, you can see that by moving the back foot it is easiest to avoid a straight-in attack whether it is a punch, a knife or a grab. It is also easy to get in a position of attack from this simple movement.

Figure 9   Figure 10

Figure 11   Figure 12

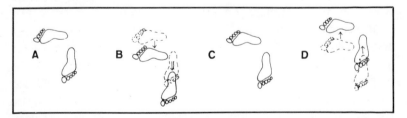

Diagrams 3A — 2B

Figure 13 and diagrams **4A-4B** show a simple 45-degree movement to the side. Notice how the feet are still fairly close together, the back is straight, and the defender is still

Figure 13   Figure 14

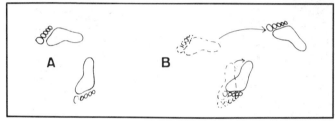

Diagrams 4A — 4B

looking at the attacker. The weight is evenly distributed on both feet. This is very important and cannot be emphasized enough. From this position it is still easy to move in any direction, and it is also easy to strike and kick. (These pictures show only one side but everything should be practiced to the opposite side also.)

Figure 14 shows a simple 90-degree movement. The body position is still the same. This position moves the body further out of the line of attack, brings one closer to the attacker and still leaves plenty of opportunities for counter-attacking.

Notice that in each of the above positions the movement with the back foot is always towards the back of the body and to the outside of the attacker's body. This is probably the safest way to move; however, that doesn't mean it is the only way. There might be times when you forget this point, or can't go that way—don't worry about it, the important thing is to move.

It is also quite acceptable to move the front foot. This can be done alone or as a part of a two-step movement. In a two-step movement the front foot moves to the side first **(15)**, and then the movement of the back foot follows **(17)**. The front foot in this case can move either way because it is only a small movement and doesn't change the alignment of the body very much. The back foot should follow very quickly, almost immediately as the front foot sets down.

Moving the front foot alone is not nearly as effective as moving both feet or the back foot only. You will almost always

Figure 15

Figure 16

Figure 17

be exposed to further attack or be turning your back to the attacker. For these reasons movement of the front foot will be limited to a 45-degree movement to the side only. Any further movement is too risky **(16)**.

So far the illustrations have shown the attack as a straight on punch. But these different ways of moving are effective against slaps, knives, grabs, or whatever, so practice moving every possible combination.

Here are a few general comments about movement. Always maintain your balance. Do not over extend the position, as this will cause you to lose balance. You can pivot on the whole foot, the heel, or the ball of the foot, whatever suits you best— it doesn't really matter. (Some karate schools say pivot only on the ball of the foot, others say the heel; just do whatever is comfortable.) Keep the weight evenly distributed as much as possible. Keep the back straight, don't just move the hips, and look up or straight ahead.

Once you have pretty much gotten the movement down from a side-facing natural stance (see fig. **4**) practice moving all these different ways from a normal stance (see fig. **3**) facing the attacker. Do this by moving one foot back or forward or even straight to the side and having the other foot follow (diags. **5A-5D**).

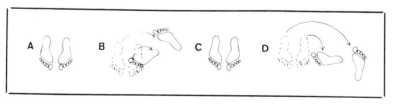

Diagrams 5A — 5B

PROTECTION WHILE MOVING

Protecting yourself while moving is very important. Remember, movement is not enough; some type of blocking with the arms and hands is necessary. But this does not have to be hard blocking. Mostly the person is concerned with protection. If you go back and study all of the previous illustrations, you will see the person being attacked has kept her hands in basically the same position. Very little movement of the hands or arms is necessary when moving out of the way of the attack. The blocking movement is mostly a second line of defense, in case the movement was a little slow or in case the attacker has changed his attack.

Going back to the basic natural stance notice the position of the arms and hands. They stay in basically this same position throughout the movement. Think of your body as moving around the arm position and you have a basic understanding of the secondary line of protection. This will be discussed further in chapter 4.

The main thing to remember is keep your eyes on the attacker and move the body and arms and hands in relation to the attacker's position. As he changes you have to respond to the change. So looking at the attacker is necessary at all times. Turning the back and ducking make it hard for you to see the attacker so these movements should be avoided as much as possible.

4

Blocks

There is a misconception among some experts that to have an effective block it is necessary to break the attacker's arm or leg. If the defender is weaker and smaller than the attacker, you can imagine what this will do to the defending person's *own* arm or leg. Even if you know how to block this way, at the very least, you will probably receive a nice big bruise. Also many people have found that "attacking" blocks are not as effective on the street. The attacker sees it coming and changes the attack. If the block isn't hard enough, the attack penetrates. That is why movement and blocking go hand-in-hand.

In any self-defense situation there is some physical pain, but it is important to minimize the amount of pain. The first concern should be with protection, and the second concern should be with absorbing as little pain as possible. So to stand there and try to break someone's arm with a block is rather senseless.

This does not mean that one is not going to get hurt while moving and blocking. The attacker might hit the arm or hand, or the defender might have to block a lead pipe or a knife, in which case the defender might end up with a broken arm or a deep cut. But better on the arms than on the head or body.

When blocking, the main thing to remember is to keep your body protected and to keep your arms and hands between you and the attacker as much as possible. An effective block is anything that disrupts the attack—the effectiveness depending on how much disruption you caused.

Look at the previous illustrations and you will notice that the front hand is always between the attacker and the defender. The close-up in figure **18** shows the approximate blocking position. Notice that the wrists of the defender and the attacker are very close. In case the defender has miscalculated a little bit

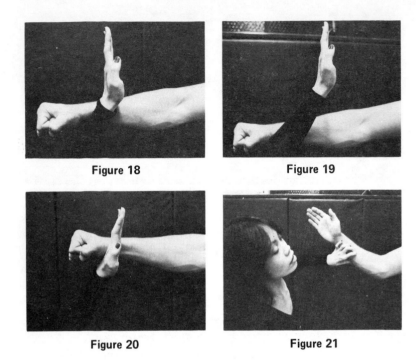

Figure 18   Figure 19

Figure 20   Figure 21

high (19) or low (20), the rest of the hand or arm is still blocking. But if the defender tries to grab the attacker's wrist and
misses, then the defender gets hit (21). Do not grab for the attacker's hand or weapon without first blocking. It is very important to block. Protect yourself. Then if there is still a possibility to grab, do so, to further disrupt the attack.

Part 2

The Best Defense Is a Good Offense

5

Strikes

Effectiveness in striking means the amount of force necessary at a certain point to end a confrontation. This can vary from slapping the attacker's face to almost killing him. How much pain an individual attacker can stand is unknown until the confrontation. Although strength will be a great help, an attacker is usually going to be stronger than the defender, so aim becomes much more important. Everyone has several vulnerable points, and it doesn't take too much strength to render a strong person almost helpless with the proper techniques. Some of the techniques are very brutal, so you must use some judgment.

The body has several effective weapons: the hands, knees, elbows, feet, fingernails, and fingers are the primary weapons, although it might be argued that the head is the most important weapon. The main areas of self-defense attack are going to be the neck and above, and the groin and below. Attacks to the body, unless aiming for a particular place such as the spine, kidneys, or solar plexus, and usually with the elbow, are generally not effective unless you have a terribly strong attack that can break ribs or double over the attacker. Because most people can't do that without several months training, this chapter will concentrate on other areas of attack.

Figures 22 and 23 show the main target areas; there are several more but they are more difficult to find. The ones shown here are easily found and quite effective. Most are easily accessible to the fists, feet, or elbows; others are smaller, and one will have to use the fingers or fingernails. Use these two pictures for reference throughout the rest of the book. When practicing, always aim for a particular point or points. Try

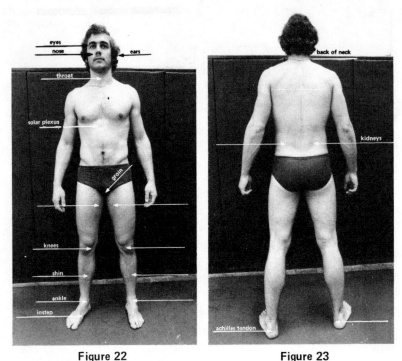

Figure 22   **Figure 23**

never to have any haphazard or unaimed strikes—they are mostly a waste of time and energy.

PUNCHING

Punches have to be well-aimed or else be very powerful to do any real damage. Figures **24, 25, 26,** and **27** show how to make a fist and how to punch. To get some weight behind the punch, it is best to step forward with the same foot as the punching hand, although stepping with the opposite foot to the punch is quite acceptable also. The best targets for a punch are the nose, eyes, throat, and groin. Punches to the body have to be very strong to be effective. This can be learned, but one should take a karate class, because most self-defense classes don't spend enough time on effective punching.

To have an effective punch the hand has to be tight. This causes some problems with people who have long fingernails (the fingernails dig into the skin of the palm). You might not want to get rid of the fingernails, because they are also good weapons, so another type of fist can be utilized (28). This type of fist is not as powerful but can be used for the same targets.

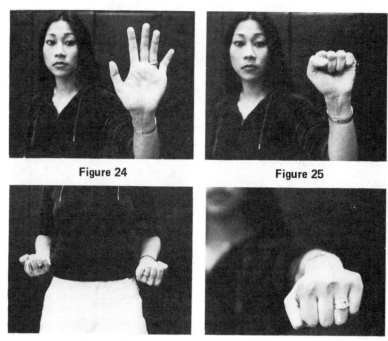

Figure 24

Figure 25

Figure 26

Figure 27

PALM HEEL

The palm heel is a very effective weapon. Figures **29** and **30** show how to make it and strike with it. The palm heel is more powerful than the fist, and there are no worries about sore knuckles, bent wrists, or fingernail cuts. The nose, eyes, groin, ears, side of head (temples), back of neck, throat, kidneys, and elbow are effective target areas. This strike is particularly effective on the face and neck, because it is very easy to open the hand up and form a claw hand with the fingers and scratch at the eyes or anywhere else on the face and neck.

ELBOW

The elbow is the most effective upper body weapon of all. It is very strong (part of the reason is because of the body weight put behind it), can go several different directions, and it is hard to block. There are several different ways to strike with

Figure 28

Figure 29

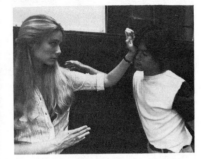

Figure 30

the elbow (figs. **31, 32**). When striking, try not to hit on the tip of the elbow unless hitting a fleshy area like the kidneys (**33**) or the solar plexus. Other areas to strike include the nose, eyes, under the jaw, neck (back and side), ear, throat, spine, and ribcage. The elbow is normally strong enough to do damage. The different ways of attacking with the elbow give the defender almost limitless means of attacking, therefore elbow strikes should take up a good share of practice time.

HANDS AND FINGERS

The hands and fingers are mainly effective for the groin, the neck and head. Hitting, grabbing, and squeezing the groin or throat are very effective things to do. Check figures **22** and **23** again, and notice the points on the neck and above. The fingers can jab and press into the hollow of the throat (fig. **34**). One can hit the windpipe and squeeze hard (**35**), or go a little higher and squeeze the carotid arteries (**36**). One can hit the nose with the palm and scratch at the eyes at the same time (**37**). Usually it is better to use a claw hand and go sideways across the eyes (**38**), as it is harder to block than a straight-in technique, plus one utilizes all of the fingers so the margin of error is less.

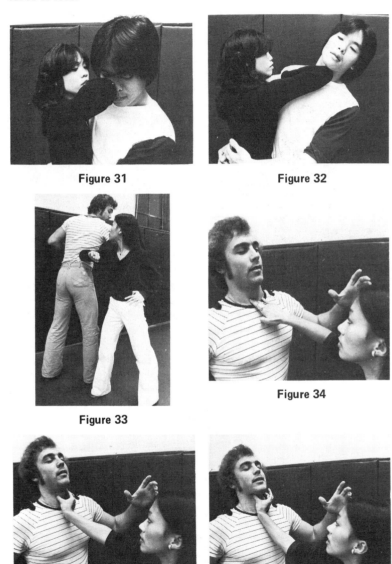

Figure 31

Figure 32

Figure 33

Figure 34

Figure 35

Figure 36

Grabbing the hair and pulling down (39) is a good tactic. If the attacker has a beard it is even easier to twist the neck and pull down. Even if the attacker is clean shaven, bald or wearing a hat, it is easy to grab the head and chin and twist quickly (40). Moving the hips to the side, hitting and grabbing the groin proves effective (41).

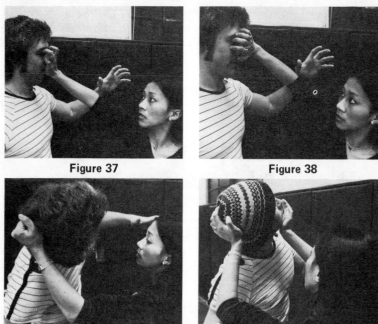

Figure 37   Figure 38

Figure 39   Figure 40

Figure 41

These are just a few of the strikes that can be utilized. Most are fairly easy to learn and do, and require little strength. They will be analyzed in more detail in chapter 9.

Remember to aim. This cannot be overstressed. If you aim for the knee and hit the thigh it will not do too much harm. Look at the pictures **(22, 23)** again. This person is fairly muscular and big (6'2" tall and over 200 pounds). If you aim for the groin and hit him in the stomach, he would just laugh at you. However, if you did hit him in the groin he definitely would not be laughing at you. He would be in pain. So aim and practice aiming all of the time.

6

Kicks

Kicking is usually a very effective self-defense technique for anyone. The difference between male and female leg strength is minimal, based on percentage of body weight. Men and women use their legs for basically the same amount of time and do practically the same things, and this has been the case from childhood through adulthood. Arm strength, on the other hand, favors the men because of the heaviness of work required. The men do most of the heavy lifting. This is still more of a cultural phenomenon than the fact that women are the so-called weaker sex. The women's movement is helping women to realize that they can do some heavy lifting or punching, and this won't be as noticeable in the future. But right now there still is this difference, and it is important to recognize it in the self-defense situation. Therefore, the legs become very important. With nearly equal leg strength, women can hold their own.

To kick effectively, you must be concerned with aiming. The main aiming points for kicks (see figs. 22, 23) are the groin, the knee (front, side, and back), the instep, shin, and ankle. Kicks higher than this are not absolutely necessary and can be dangerous unless one practices high kicks and goes to a karate or tae kwon do class to learn the proper ways of kicking. This chapter is concerned with four types of kicks; the front kick, low side kick, knee kick, and heel kick for close-in encounters.

FRONT KICK

The front kick is a very easy and effective kick. There are four basic movements: up, out, back, and down (figs. 42, 43, 44, 45). Each of these movements is important. Bringing the leg up helps to cock the leg and causes the kick to go straight out into the target rather than sliding up into it. Bringing it

back to the cocked position is faster and less dangerous (harder
to grab) than just letting the leg fall down, plus one can kick
again from this position.

From the basic defensive posture it is important to be able to
kick with both legs fast and easily (another reason for the even
weight balance). First practice kicking in the stances, then
practice moving and kicking (**46**). This kick is also effective if
one doesn't have time or room to move. As the attacker moves
toward the defender, raise the arms for blocking and kick
straight ahead at one of the target areas (**47**).

Figure 43

Figure 42

Figure 44

Figure 45

Figure 46

Figure 47

SIDE KICK

The side kick is very effective for close-in encounters. Although it is a very powerful kick even when used above the waist level, it is a more difficult kick to learn, and so its uses will be confined to the knee and below. This kick also has a four-count movement: up, out, back, and down (figs. 48, 49, 50, 51). The heel of the foot is used quite effectively against the knee, shin, ankle, and instep (52).

KNEE KICK

The knee kick—raising the knee quickly into the target area— also is effective for close-in encounters. The target areas will vary, depending mostly upon the attacker's height and the defender's height. The groin, thigh and kidneys are possible target areas (53). If the attacker is bent over, the head also becomes a good target (54).

Another very effective kick is with the heel to the shins, especially close-in. First raise the leg up with the knee to the side, then come smashing out and down on the shin with the heel (55). It looks somewhat like a soccer kick.

One important thing to consider in these situations is that one cannot concentrate only on an offensive move or moves. One always has to be aware of defense. Keep the arms (or free arm) up for blocking purposes. Always keep the attacker in sight and be aware of his possible lines of attack. Go back and study the blocking positions to see some of the ways of protecting the body while doing the counter techniques. This will be covered in more detail in chapters 9 and 10.

Kicks are very effective, and if you can distract the attacker with the hands up high while kicking low, the sudden pain on the lower part of the attacker's body can surprise the attacker and give the defender a slight edge; so make the most of it.

Figure 48

Figure 49

Figure 50

Figure 51

Figure 52

Figure 53

Figure 54

Figure 55

7
Falls

Learning how to fall is very important. If hit and knocked down by an attacker, you do not want to double the chances of injury by being hurt a second time from the fall. The most important part of the body is the head; it is not protected by muscles or surrounded by adipose tissue. If the head hits the ground from a fall, it might knock the person unconscious, make her dizzy or disoriented, or possibly even cause death. The back of the head, just above the neck is probably more important to protect than the front or side, because it contains the body's breathing center. If this center is hit hard enough, the shock might temporarily paralyze the action of the breathing center.

If you are hit, you want to fall, so as not to be hurt further. There are several ways to fall and most are based on the idea of absorbing the shock of landing over as large a surface area as possible. The best way to do this is to roll out of the fall in the direction of the fall.

FORWARD ROLLS

Figures **56** and **57** show how to roll forward if pushed or hit from behind. The main thing to remember as you are rolling is to get both hands down and decide which arm to roll over. Spread the shock of the fall over the hands, arms, back, and legs. Keep the head protected by tucking the chin and looking to the opposite side of the arm over which you are rolling. Notice that the head never touches the ground and also that the arms and legs protect the body as much as possible as you roll. Try to learn the roll; a slapping fall is fine in a mat room but might break an arm or ankle out on concrete streets or sidewalks.

Figure 56   **Figure 57**

AFTER THE FALL

What happens after the fall? Should you attempt to get up or stay down? Ideally you should never fall, but unfortunately, you cannot always have an ideal situation. If you do fall and roll, the time to get up is right then by continuing the roll, either forwards or backwards. You are usually in a better position when standing on both feet and able to move around freely. If you are on the ground, it is more difficult to move and you will be at a disadvantage. If there is more than one attacker, definitely attempt to get up out of the roll, otherwise there is too much of a disadvantage when on the ground.

If you fall, be aware of where the attacker is as you are getting up. Get up rapidly and face the attacker as quickly as possible (58) and protect yourself while getting up. The head should be protected the most as it is the most vulnerable and the easiest part of the body for the attacker to hit.

If you cannot get up, or are too slow—perhaps you passed out momentarily and awoke to find the attacker very close—it might be best to stay down. Figure 59 shows one of the negative possibilities in an attempt to get up when it was not feasible to do so. If you are down, think about protecting your body. In this case get the legs up between you and the attacker (60). The pivot point will be the buttocks. Use the arms to turn in either direction (61). By continuous *fast* kicking you should be able to ward off the attack. Do not let the attacker grab the legs. The way to overcome someone who is down is to get to the side of the person and fall on the side of the legs (62). (This is mentioned so that if you are the one that is down you know what to avoid.)

Several big men have said that all they would have to do is jump on the legs and that would crush the woman. But it is just about impossible for a man to do this. A woman's legs are strong and all she has to do is keep her legs up when the attacker jumps (63) and then move them to the side. The attacker falls to the side (64), and the woman rolls away and gets up.

If you do fall, protect the head, attempt to roll out of the fall, and get to a standing position again. If that isn't possible, stay on the ground and keep the attacker away with the legs. You might skin your hands, arms and buttocks, and tear the clothing, but that is better than most alternatives.

Figure 58

Figure 59

Figure 60

Figure 61

Figure 62

Figure 63

Figure 64

The best thing to do is to take a judo, aikido, hapkido, wrestling or gymnastics tumbling class so that you learn how to fall properly. This short chapter cannot teach the reader the proper techniques. Basically all it can do is to advise you of how important it is to learn to fall properly.

8

Throws

Most throws that do not involve one of the attacker's joints (wrist, elbow, or neck) are fairly useless in a street situation. This statement will probably make judo people and wrestlers angry, but an explanation will be attempted. First, judo is a sport and as such most people rarely use it as a self-defense technique. In the few places where it is practiced as self-defense, it is used against others who know how to fall and know how they are going to be thrown so attacker-resistance usually isn't there. Judo as practiced now is done within weight categories which should tell you something right there. The weight categories were instituted because added weight and strength are a definite advantage in judo competition. In other words, with equal skills the bigger and stronger person is going to win. On the street the person attacking is almost always going to be bigger and stronger, so to attempt to throw this person to the ground is not the wisest thing you can do.

To accomplish a throw one usually has to use both hands or arms and put the feet in the proper position. In other words, both legs and both arms are tied up in attempting a throw against a bigger and stronger attacker who is resisting as much as possible. Maybe the throw will work, but it is not worth the effort or danger involved. This is even more true when there are two or more attackers. For these reasons, other easier-to-learn methods that don't require so much emphasis on strength are recommended. If you are interested in learning throws, or even just the mechanics behind them, go to a judo or wrestling class.

9

Integrating the Different Techniques

In any type of counter-attack, aiming is very important. Most of the time you will be weaker than the attacker, and unless the counters are aimed very precisely, you will be wasting time and energy. Aiming is easily learned; it just takes practice. You can put a life-size picture on the wall and aim at the vital points or just practice kicking and striking at any life-size object. If you kick for the groin and hit the hip, it will certainly hurt, but it won't stop the attacker; it will only make him more angry and more wary—so don't miss.

When counter-attacking, you should realize that most times one strike or one kick is not going to be enough. Several rapid attacks at the vital points—simultaneously aware of your own defense—are going to be necessary. Some attackers can absorb a lot of punishment, and, being stronger, all they need is one blow to really damage or knock out the defender. Be prepared to fight, and remember to protect the body while doing so. If the tide is going against you, give serious consideration to going for a very vulnerable area—usually the eyes—to save yourself. This is a very important decision and is one that only you can make. If you are winning, then try to get away as fast as possible. Don't press your luck, or skill.

Always defend yourself as vigorously as possible; do not go half-heartedly, because this will tend to make the attacker more violent without accomplishing anything for your own benefit, i.e., getting away or stopping the attacker.

STRAIGHT-IN ATTACKS

Straight-in attacks are tactics such as: punching (jabs, upper-cuts, or karate punches), pushing, or a stabbing motion with a

47

knife (weapon defenses will be covered in chapter 10). The initial response is to move out of the way, preferably to the outside of the attacker's arm (as this is the safest), and to get the hands up for protection. From this position, depending on how the defender has stepped and how close she is to the attacker, an attempt at a counter-attack should be made.

Figures 65–67 show a two-step or one-step movement to the outside while remaining close to the attacker. From here, slide the right arm up and hit the attacker in the nose, or, in a more dangerous situation, use a claw hand and go for the eyes (65), or grab the attacker's hair and pull *straight down* and kick (do not pull the hair back, as this is not very effective) (66). If the defender is short, and the attacker is tall, one can easily elbow the rib cage (67). After counter-attack, run away or follow up with more kicks and strikes.

Figures 68–70 show the same pattern of movement to the outside, but this time the defender is farther away. Use either leg to kick at the knee (68, 69) or rib cage (70). The knee is the safest target, and remember to keep the head and hands up.

Sometimes, perhaps, you won't be able to move, such as in a between-parked-cars situation. Just throw up the hands in front of the body to reduce the target area and kick for the knees (71), groin (72), or go for the throat, grab and squeeze (73).

Figure 65

Figure 66

Figure 67

Figure 68

Figure 69

Figure 70

CIRCULAR ATTACKS

Circular attacks consist mainly of slaps, knockout punches, or the swinging of a weapon or a knife. How the defender will move is determined mostly by the closeness of the attack. If you are very close, move inside towards the attacker; if fairly far away, move away and let the swing go by. If it is aimed right at the head and the defender can't move or doesn't have time, get the hands up and stop the blow by blocking it with the arms. This hurts the arms somewhat, but better there than the head.

Figure 71   Figure 72

Figure 73

For a close-in slap or punch, take two steps as in figures **74** and **75**. Now the defender will be moving away from the slap or punch and towards the attacker. From here one can use any of the counters shown in figures **65** to **73**, plus an elbow to the face (**76**) or the side of the fist to the throat (**77**). Figure **78** shows a step in, with the nearest foot to the slap. From here use any of the possible counters. The throat and groin are especially good targets with the hand and knee, respectively.

Figure **79** shows a block against the arm when one hasn't moved. After the block, counter with a kick (**80**) or strike to the throat (**81**), nose, or eyes.

GRABS

When an attacker grabs, he is usually attempting to set the

victim up for a strike, to pull or push in a certain direction, or to pin a part of the body. It is not always the grab itself that you have to worry about. After all, if an attacker grabs you, he can do nothing else with that hand at that moment. When someone grabs you, your main concern is what he is doing with, or has in, the other hand. The response is the same: move, get the hand(s) up, and counter. The main concern is protection, so block and counter-strike as quickly as possible.

Figure 74

Figure 75

Figure 76

Figure 77

Figure 78

Figure 79

Figure 80

Figure 81

You should always be alert enough to realize when someone is approaching close enough to grab you. The first line of defense is movement. Figures 82 and 83 show simple ways of avoiding grabs. Notice that the woman moves the hands away (82), turns the shoulders, gets the hands up to interfere with the grab, and is always in a position to kick or strike (83). The same principles apply if grabbed from behind; move, spin, get the hands up, and strike (84, 85). These movements all have to be done fast, and the easiest way to practice is to have someone attempt to grab you anywhere while you try to avoid the grab.

If you are grabbed and the hold is not very strong, or the person has already started moving, continue the movement and strike to take the attacker's mind off the grab and put in on the painful area. If one can make the attacker reach farther than he had planned to get a good hold, it is to the defender's advantage (86), because the attacker is somewhat off balance and more vulnerable to a counter-attack (87).

There will probably be times, however, when the attacker does get a good grip. When this happens, you will have to be concerned with the attacker's free hand as well as the gripping

Figure 82

Figure 83

Figure 84

Figure 85

hand. First to be discussed will be how to get out of the grab, and then how to avoid a strike while being held. The weakest point of a grip is the area between the thumb and the fingers,

Figure 86

Figure 87

Figure 88

so the movement should be towards the thumb **(88).** The weakest fingers are the little and ring fingers. These two points
are the bases for your releasing from a grab.

Figure 89

Before discussing how to release, it is important to keep a clear head and not panic just because someone bigger and stronger has grabbed you. Easy to say—yes. Easy to do—not quite. To tighten up and make wild attempts to pull away from the attacker is to waste time and energy. You simply have to divert the attacker's attention, determine how to get out, and do it.

One of my students who had been grabbed as she was walking home one night stated that there was no time to react and she couldn't think. It is difficult to react coolly, but by knowing what to do, practicing it, and being aware of the surrounding environment, you can learn to react in a less panic-stricken way. To get the attacker into thinking about something else (pain), hit or kick anywhere, but especially the head, groin, legs and feet. The pain he feels will get his mind off the grip.

Sometimes, your hit won't have to be that hard; the attack itself will make the attacker think about avoiding the counterattack, giving you an opportunity to get out. Some basic principles include moving the whole body in the direction one wants to go (89). Many people attempt to yank the shoulder or arms away, but if the defender is smaller or weaker than the attacker, using arm strength alone—even if the attacker is distracted with the blows—is pretty much useless. (Figures **90**, **91** show the wrong ways to move.) After kicking or striking, determine which way to go by either breaking out against the thumb or pulling the little finger away and then breaking out (**92**). This whole sequence should be instantaneous.

Figure 90

Figure 91

Figure 92

Figures **93** through **107** show several wrist grab counters. For the purposes of brevity it will be understood that the person being grabbed has already kicked or hit as the first movements and will also continue to kick or strike while attempting to release, and after effecting the release. When practicing (try to get a partner), have your partner grab about one-half strength at first until you get the motion and ideas down. Then as you get better, speed up the grab and the strength of the grab.

Figure **93** shows a same side grab with the defender pulling any of the fingers or thumb away. One can also press the first joint of any of the fingers up into the second joint if the person is making a fist (**94**). Figure **95** shows a step and twist away from the attacker going to the outside of his body while kicking. Figure **96** shows a throat grab and step and twist while going across the front of the attacker.

Figure 93

Figure 94

The following figures illustrate cross-arm grabs. Working against the fingers as in **93** and **94** causes the same reaction.

Figure 95

Figure 96

Figure 97

Figure **97** shows a step to the outside and smash to the elbow with the palm heel either breaking or hitting up and turning

Figure 98

Figure 99

Figure 100

the elbow over (98).

If the attacker grabs both of your wrists with both of his

Figure 101

Figure 102

hands, concentrate on only one of the hands and get out as in any of the above ways. Realize that the attacker can't do much here, as both of his hands are tied up also. After kicking or spitting in his face, bring the hands together while moving in one direction and break out (**99**).

If the attacker grabs both wrists with one of his hands (**100**), (you should never allow this to happen), then turn away from his free hand (**101**) to keep from getting hit and kick the nearest knee or ankle (**102**).

If an attacker grabs one wrist from behind (**103**), spin quickly in that direction, bring up the free hand for protection (**104**), and strike (**105**).

If the attacker grabs both wrists from behind, keep the wrists there, pivot the body by bending the arms until sideways to the

Figure 103

Figure 104

Figure 105

attacker (**106**), and kick the knee or groin (**107**).

The same principles apply to arm grabs. First kick or strike,

Figure 106

Figure 107

Figure 108

then move. You can grab the finger(s) and pull away or push as above (**93, 94**). Other counters include making a circle of the arm and coming across the attacker's arm (**108**). You can circle

Figure 109

Figure 110

in either direction **(109)** until the attacker lets go or is set up for another kick or strike **(110)**. It doesn't matter if your arm(s) are grabbed from the front, side or back. All of these techniques work on the same principle no matter where the attacker grabs.

If the attacker grabs across the body **(111)**, step to the outside of his arm and strike the elbow while holding on to his hand with the other free hand **(112)**.

Grabs from behind with one arm usually pull the defender back **(113)**. Spin quickly, get both arms up for protection **(114)**, then strike **(115)**.

If the attacker grabs your shoulders from behind **(116)**, raise one arm up high **(117)**, step back with that same foot **(118)**, and come across and down on the attacker's arm **(119)**.

Most hapkido, jui jitsu, and aikido martial arts emphasize

Figure 111

Figure 112

Figure 113

various releases and joint locks or throws off of these types of
grabs, and it is recommended that you take some lessons to

Figure 114

Figure 115

Figure 116

get a feel for these movements and techniques. These martial arts usually only pay lip service to the striking and kicking

Figure 117

Figure 118

Figure 119

Figure 120

Figure 121

Figure 122

techniques preliminary to doing the techniques. It is recommended that these preliminary movements are of the utmost importance and should be an integral part of the techniques.

Body grabs should be avoided at all costs. They are difficult to get out of, and you are definitely in a bad position. You should move out of the way as soon as you feel threatened. However, there might be times when you can't avoid this position. In these cases there are still certain things to do. A body grab will usually be from the front or back and will sometimes pin the arms, which is definitely to be avoided. So if you can't avoid the grab, at least try to keep one arm free.

Figure 123

Figure 124

Figure 125

Figure 126

If you can keep your arms free, the following figures show what to do from the front, back, and side.

From the front you can do several things, such as: slap the ears (120), grab the hair and pull down (121), hit the throat (122), squeeze the windpipe (123), twist the neck (124), scratch the eyes (125), or hit the nose (126). Most of these defenses can be done from the side also, and it doesn't matter whether or not the attacker lifts the person off of the ground.

If you are attacked from behind, you can do the following

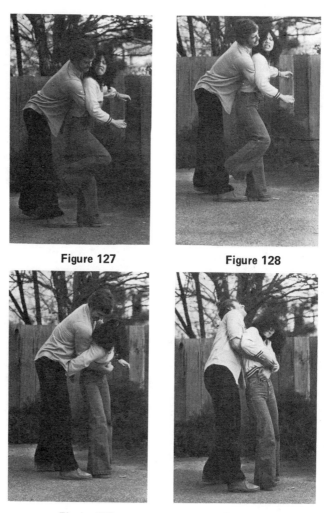

Figure 127   Figure 128

Figure 129   Figure 130

things: kick the knee (127), and scrape down the shin to the instep (128), move the hips to the side and strike the groin (129). One can work on the fingers again (130), or if the arms are long enough, reach back and scratch the eyes or grab the hair (131).

If both arms are pinned, you have to rely more on leg and body movement from an awkward position. This applies whether the feet are on the ground or whether the attacker has lifted the person off the ground. If the attacker grabs you from

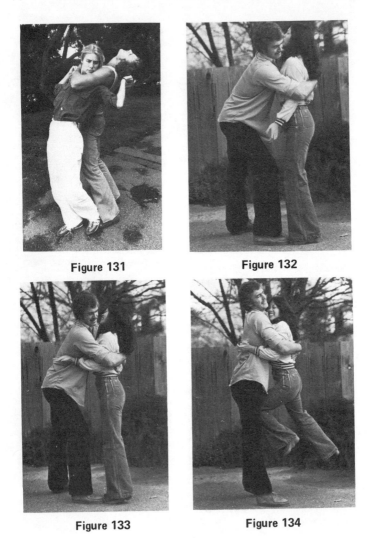

Figure 131

Figure 132

Figure 133

Figure 134

the front and pins both arms as in figure 132, inhale and expand the chest and hit just below the short ribs on the side (133), knee the groin (134), pinch the insides of the thighs (135), or bite the neck or shoulder (136). Bites can be very, very painful and should be used whenever possible.

When grabbed from behind (fig. 137), work on the fingers

Figure 135

Figure 136

Figure 137

Figure 138

while kicking **(138)** and stomping on the feet **(139)**. (Do several tactics simultaneously, rather than one at a time.) When stomping, don't pick your foot up too high, because you might lose your balance; just a little bit is very effective. Also throw the head back into the attacker's nose if tall enough to do this. You can also try to move the hips to the side again **(140)** and

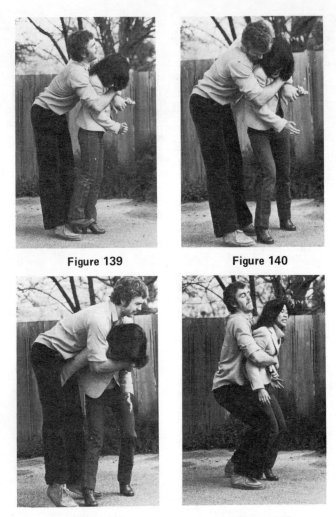

Figure 139   Figure 140

Figure 141   Figure 142

grab the groin (141). If you are picked up from behind, immediately throw the hips forward (142) and turn to the side as
much as possible (143), and strike the groin (144).

If an attacker grabs you with one hand and attempts to hit
you with his other hand or is using a weapon, first think about
protection. It makes no sense to try to get out of the hold while

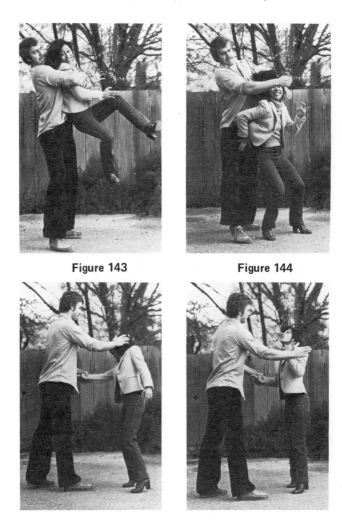

Figure 143   **Figure 144**

Figure 145   **Figure 146**

the attacker is knocking you out **(145).** Be aware of the attacker's other hand and move first to protect against that hand or weapon in that hand. Get the hand up and move as far away from the striking hand as possible. Make it hard for the attacker to hit. Whenever the opportunity is present, kick low, or hit high. You can distract him by spitting in his face **(146),** kicking

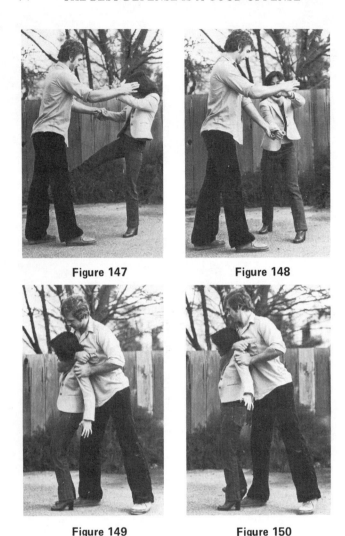

Figure 147

Figure 148

Figure 149

Figure 150

low (147), and then getting loose (148) and getting away. Here the defense is to protect with block(s), kick, and get loose.

CHOKES

To release from a rear choke, first keep the chin down and towards the elbow (149) (do not raise the chin up gasping for air), stomp on the instep of the attacker's foot (150) and do

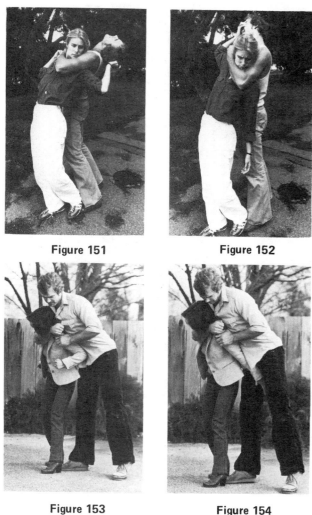

Figure 151

Figure 152

Figure 153

Figure 154

any or all of the following: if the arms are long enough reach back and scratch the face and eyes (152), or fake this and grab the hair and pull down to the side (151), if shorter move to the side, elbow the solar plexus (153), strike the groin and squeeze (154), grab the attacker's finger or thumb and pull until it

Figure 155

Figure 156

Figure 157

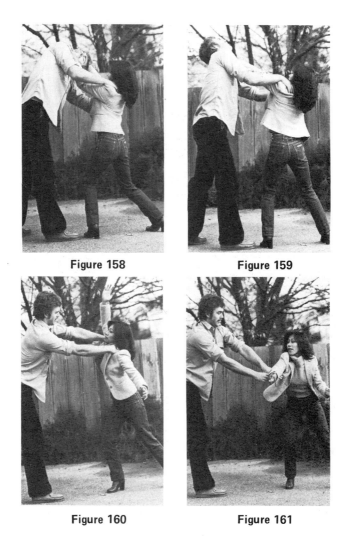

Figure 158

Figure 159

Figure 160

Figure 161

breaks or his arm comes away (155), pinch the inside of the attacker's thighs, as this is a very sensitive area (156). Repeat any of the above as necessary.

Figure 157 shows a front choke. It is relatively easy to get out of this hold. Grab the little fingers and pull apart while kicking or punching; if close enough, grab the head and twist (158), hit the throat hard (159), raise one arm up, pretend to be an airplane and turn one way (160) while stepping backward to release (161), or hit the elbows together, push up, and

Figure 162

Figure 163

Figure 164

step back (162).

In a rear choke you can do almost the same things. Pull the fingers apart while kicking **(163)**, step back and low while hitting the rib cage or the solar plexus with the elbow, step back and bring the arm under **(164)** and then over the attacker's arms **(165, 166)**.

NONSTANDING POSITIONS

So far, the discussion has centered on what to do if attacked while in a standing or walking position. There might be some instances however, when you will be attacked while lying or sitting down. Your movement will be much more limited, but

Figure 165   **Figure 166**

you will still be able to block and counter just as easily most of the time.

Sitting

You may worry about these kind of attacks while in a car. (If you are not in a car, you should be able to block and stand up fairly easily; the movement is not too limited in this case.) The attacker will either be to the side or behind. You can avoid this situation entirely by looking in the back seat before getting in the car and driving with the car doors locked. In the summertime keep only the driver's window open if at all possible.

Hitchhiking

If you are picked up hitchhiking and find yourself going where you don't want to go, try to get out at the first opportunity. Always take note of the license plate number before getting in the car, and make the driver notice you doing it.

When the attacker is in the passenger seat and you are driving you might try such tactics as:

- suddenly slamming on the brakes (in hopes the attacker hits his head on the windshield)

- cornering sharply to knock him off balance. In both cases get out of the car quickly and run away. (It is best to do this near a populated area, so there will be plenty of people around.)

Figure 167

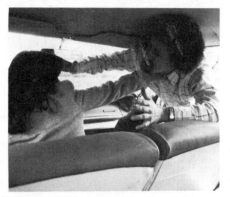

Figure 168

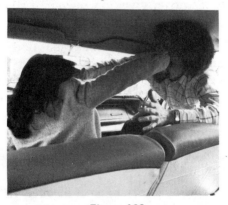

Figure 169

Figure 170

Figure 171

• driving to a police station, fire station, or emergency room of a hospital. This is also true if someone is following in a car. *Don't drive home.*

An attacker grabbing at you from the side can be kept away by holding the hands up and always moving around his face. Attempt to hit the nose **(167)**, the throat **(168)**, pull the hair or scratch the eyes **(169)**. Try to get the legs up between you and the attacker and just keep kicking **(170)**.

If the attacker is behind, turn and face him and do the same as above **(171)**, or just reach back and scratch the eyes and pull

Figure 172

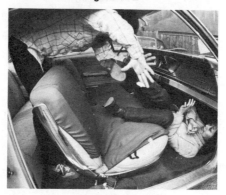

Figure 173

the hair (172). If the car is big enough, slide down on the floor
with the legs up and kick (173). This won't be comfortable or
modest, but it will be very hard for an attacker to hit you
except on the legs, or to pull you out. If there are weapons
involved, you will not be able to do some of these things.
Weapons will be discussed in more detail in chapter 10.

It is best to be in an upright position and to regain that
position if one is down, without jeopardizing protection. Because that isn't always possible one has to learn how to protect
oneself while on the ground. If a person is thrown down or falls
down and lands on the front part of the body, immediately
roll over and get the legs and arms up. The worst possible way
to face an attacker is to be lying down on your stomach. The
possibilities of defense are sorely limited. Being on the back

Figure 174

is much better—at least the hands and legs can serve as a defense.

In chapter 7 it was shown what to do if one is down on the ground, on the back, and the attacker is not on top. The same chapter talked about how to fall so that you don't get hurt from the fall itself. By kicking vigorously and continuously and pivoting you should be able to keep the attacker away.

If the attacker gets on top (perhaps you are sleeping), the attacker is going to have a definite advantage in strength and weight. Movement and avoidance are impossible, so resist with all your resources, courage, and deception (chapter 11).

If you are on your back with the attacker on top, you will have to worry about being grabbed and/or hit. The attacker will probably try to pin the arms and hit. If he just pins the arms with both his hands (174), concentrate on getting just one arm free by using circular movements and striking for the targets on the throat and face. If he is in this position, he can't do too much harm. Both of his hands are tied up holding yours so he can't strike. The main problems occur when he is holding one of your arms and hitting with the free hand, or, even worse, if he is holding both arms with one of his hands. In this position you must get one hand free at all costs and attempt to cover the head with the upper arms so he can't hit very effectively (175).

If an attacker is on top, you must protect your body and attempt at every opportunity to strike him in a vital area and get him off. If one hand is free, block and strike for the throat

Figure 175

Figure 176

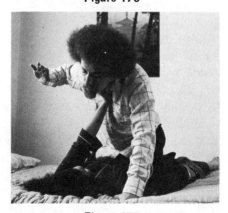

Figure 177

and push back (**176**), grab the windpipe and squeeze (**177**), grab the hair and pull (**178**), or hit the groin.

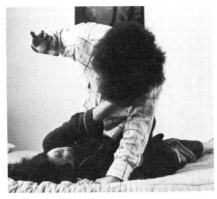

Figure 178

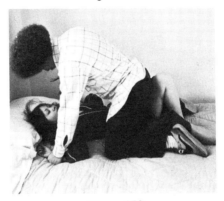

Figure 179

Figure 180
Getting the attacker off should be done at the same time
as these strikes. First bend one leg (**179**), raise the hips *high*
(this is very important) (**180**), and turn quickly to the opposite

Figure 181

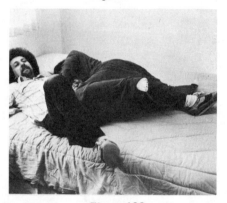

Figure 182

Figure 183

side of the bent leg (181). Follow up with a knee to the groin
(182). It doesn't really matter how the attacker is sitting or

Figure 184

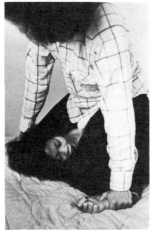

Figure 185

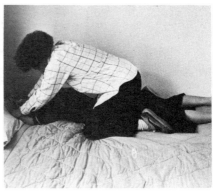

Figure 186

kneeling while on top. Even if the attacker is kneeling on the arms (see figure 183), you can still pivot to one side. First grab the legs hard, lift the hips high and pivot (184). Also, you can bite the inside of the thighs (185), a very sensitive area, as hard as possible.

If you are on your stomach and the attacker is on top you are at an even greater disadvantage. The first movement should be to attempt to draw the arms (186) and legs (187) under-

Figure 187

Figure 188

neath the body. Next, roll over to one side (188) and do an
elbow strike while rolling over (189). If the attacker has his

Figure 189

Figure 190

arms around your body, grab the fingers and break (**190**). The main concern is to get him off and roll to one side so that he falls or rolls over also. The defender should turn rapidly on to the back or side (facing the attacker) so that the legs and hands can be used more effectively.

Sometimes an attacker will attempt to kick the victim. Fortunately, most attackers have not had any formal karate, kung-fu, or tae kwon do training so that the kicks are not as effective as they could be. Most street type of kicks are low and in more of a swinging manner (**191**) than regular martial art kicks. The easiest way to block these type of kicks is to just put the side of the foot (as in a side kick) in the path of the

Figure 191

Figure 192

Figure 193

Figure 194

attacker's shin (192). But, first, attempt to move out of the path of the kick totally (193). Whatever you do, do not attempt to reach down and block the kick with the arms or hands (194). All this does is bring the head lower and closer to the attacker, something that no defender wants.

10

Weapons

Any time weapons are involved in a self-defense situation, the picture suddenly changes. The probability of a person getting hurt is now much higher. The attacker who uses a weapon is saying that he has absolutely no regard for your life.

In a robbery or rape the attacker usually wants a specific thing. He doesn't necessarily want to kill or maim the victim. But anyone who uses a weapon does not think that way. To kill or maim wouldn't bother this type of person in the least. To stop the attack you might have to resort to downright brutal methods. Perhaps you feel that this goes against your nature, that by reacting in a brutal manner you are coming down to the attacker's level. However, it is better to fight and save yourself at whatever level than to be killed and die a needless death. By doing the projection exercises recommended in chapter 2, you will be able to cope with more brutal responses if the situation should occur.

The main target areas are the eyes, knees, with the throat and groin as secondary targets. Anything else is usually a waste of time (although pulling the hair can be effective sometimes). You want to put the attacker in so much pain quickly that he can't continue the action. The defender should attempt to end the confrontation immediately. The eyes and knees are the best target areas, because they are easily accessible and damage there causes so much pain that the attacker can't do anything. The throat and groin are also good targets, but not as easily accessible, and it takes a harder blow to do enough damage to stop the attacker. A scratch on the eye is enough to stop the attack.

This chapter will be concerned with weapon defenses against guns, knives and striking instruments from standing, prone, and sitting positions. It will also discuss what you can use as defense weapons and how to use these implements.

WEAPON DEFENSES
Against Blunt Instruments

First to be considered are the striking implements such as a lead pipe, a piece of wood, or an umbrella. Striking instruments (lead pipe, wood, umbrella) can be used either in a straight-in attack (pokes, jabs) or in a swinging attack. In either case the pattern of defense is the same: move, block, and strike. For straight-in attacks, move to one side or the other, keeping the arms up to block. The stepping pattern is the same as a straight-in attack without a weapon. This movement is also the same with a straight-in knife stab (195, 196, 197). The defender will

Figure 195

Figure 196

Figure 197

have to use extra caution and make sure she is always protected in some way. It doesn't help to move, block once, and then strike while leaving the body unprotected, because at that instant you are vulnerable and a weapon can do more damage than just a hand strike.

An attack from above, but still essentially straight, is avoidable in the same way. The only difference is that the hands are held higher (**198**). One still moves to the side (**199**), blocks, and counters.

Most of the attacks with these types of weapons are going to be in some type of swinging pattern with a slight downward angle, somewhat like a slapping motion. The length of the weapon, the defender's position, and the attacker's position, will determine whether the defender moves away or in. If the

Figure 198

Figure 199

Figure 200

Figure 201

weapon is relatively short, then step back and lean back slightly—*do not duck* (200). If it is a long weapon and you don't feel

Figure 202

Figure 203

you can get out of range, it is probably better to move in and attack. In other words, get in close enough so that the person is blocking the arm and able to strike to the vulnerable areas (201).

One can use either a simple pivot (202) as you practiced before, or a two-step pattern (203, 204) to block the arm. The arm block will have to be fairly strong and you might receive bruises on the arm, but that is better than a cracked skull. One must aim for the attacker's wrist to block (205). This allows a margin of error on either side in case of miscalculation. Do not block the upper arm only, as the attacker has merely to bend his arm at the elbow to hit (206). From this position you have the following openings: fist to nose, fingers to eyes, knee to groin, elbow to head (207), kick to knee or foot stomp (208). It is recom-

Figure 204

Figure 205

Figure 206

mended that the defender hit high, then low, high, middle, or some other similar pattern. If one concentrates only on high

Figure 207

counters, then the attacker will probably be able to block several of the blows, because his mind and energy is focused there. By going high, low, high, middle, etc., the attacker never gets a chance to coordinate his mind and blocks. The defender now stands a better chance of being more effective and ending the danger.

Against Knives

Confronting a knife is perhaps one of our strongest instinctual fears. Fortunately, most attackers are unskilled with this weapon. Many police officers relate that knife attacks are frequently executed in a downward slash, which is probably the result of our exposure to television and movies. It is fairly easy to block this type of attack. What you want to do is to take one cut, if you have to, on the arms, and not on the throat, ribcage, or abdomen.

There seems to be a tendency to grab at the knife hand, using the grab as a block. This is a very dangerous maneuver to attempt. First move, block, and then, if possible, attempt to grab the knife hand. If you attempt a grab and miss, you may get cut, because a grab with the hand is only blocking about six inches of body area. A block with one arm offers fifteen to eighteen inches of protection, and a block with both arms offers up to three feet of protection (211). So don't sacrifice all of this protection with a high-risk attempt at a grab.

Defense against a downward slash involves moving to the outside or inside of the attacker with the hands held high

Figure 208

Figure 209

Figure 210

(209) and kicking to the knee or groin (210). One will have to
concentrate on keeping the hands and arms between the knife

Figure 211

Figure 212

and the body at all times. To do this, the blocking arms start high and one of them comes down as the knife comes down (211), otherwise the defender leaves the whole side of the body defenseless (212). If you are strong enough or don't have time to move, raise both hands up over the head, keeping the hands a few inches apart (213), and kick with the foot (214).

Several schools of martial arts recommend an x-block (215), and it can be very effective. It is not recommended here because it leaves half of the body open plus it is easier to overwhelm one line of defense, even if stronger, than two lines of defense. With a one-arm line of defense, you will slow down and hinder the attacker somewhat, but one more line of defense with the other arm will hinder the attack twice as much.

Figure 213

Figure 214

Figure 215

Figure 216

Figure 217

If the attacker stabs straight ahead, you can use any of the simple movement patterns to the side that were shown previously with straight-in attacks.

A horizontal slashing motion is one of the most difficult attacks to block; most people have a tendency to block too high (**216**) and then get cut under the block. The best way to avoid this is to stay as far away as possible from the attacker. Keep the hands up and continue moving back and to the side. *Do not stop moving.* To start from a flat-footed position and move quickly is much more difficult than to continue moving once started, as any tennis or basketball player will tell you. The best target area is usually the knee as the attacker steps forward (**217**). The time to attack is as the knife passes by and before it comes back with the outside of the arm facing the defender

Figure 218

(218). This is an easier block and allows a greater margin for error than when the knife is coming from the other direction.

The movement should always be away from the knife. If you can't move back or want to end the confrontation, the only alternative is to move in. *Move in and to the side away from the slashing motion,* as in the two-step side moving pattern described in chapter 3.

Pulling the hair can be very effective. It is painful, and where the head goes the rest of the body follows. Grab as much hair as possible and pull it all the way to the ground (you should squat, not bend at the waist). The attacker's body will follow with a hard fall. After doing these counters, continue moving away in the same direction.

Against a good knife fighter there are only two areas of counter-attack—the eyes and the knees. To go for anything else is to risk serious injury. You will more likely get cut, but take the cut on the arms and end the fight immediately. The defender must wait for the right time to move and then move decisively; any hesitation will cause serious injury.

How do you recognize a good knife fighter? There are several ways: (1) He is very patient, (2) he does not try to stab, and (3) he does not make big motions—the knife is always out in front of him, and the other hand is close by for protection. This type of fighter just attempts to slice and nick. Pretty soon, after many little cuts, the defender will get pretty discouraged, weak, and tired from loss of blood. Then the good knife fighter might become a little more aggressive, but mostly he just wears the

Figure 219

Figure 220

defender down until she has lost too much blood to fight, or he waits for the defender to make a mistake and then cuts quickly.

Not a pretty picture, which is why if one is ever in this position, first wait for him to make the move **(219)**, then if the opportunity is present, move in, take the cut on the arms and attack the eyes **(220)** (or pull the hair down if you can't bring yourself to do the more deadly and brutal techniques **(221)**. If you are tall enough, keep the arms up and kick the knee. If you can break the knee, he can't come foward any more and you have the opportunity to run away. Hopefully, you will never meet this type of attacker. The most common knife attacks probably look fairly easy after this, but be very careful and treat the knife with respect, and constantly be aware of where it is in any confrontation.

Figure 221

Figure 222

If the attacker is pointing a knife at the front of your throat and also holding you in some manner (222), there is basically one thing to do, which is fairly risky. First raise the free arm up between the body and the knife while simultaneously stepping sideways away from the knife (223), then counter-attack. This can be done subtly (with distractions like talking or crying) or fast and violently. As can be seen, this is risky, but if you are in this situation it is not going to be easy to get out. The use of deception and other nonphysical ways to get out of these types of situations are discussed in chapter 11.

The other great fear in a knife attack is an attack from behind with a knife at the throat (224). You should be able to avoid this situation. About the only way to have any chance of getting out of this is to move as you see the knife coming to the

Figure 223

Figure 224

Figure 225

throat. If you do see the knife coming to the throat, get the hands up (**225**) and duck under the attacker's knife hand armpit

Figure 226

Figure 227

Figure 228

(226), and move away (227). Other than this method, which is undeniably risky and requires a lot of practice, it might be

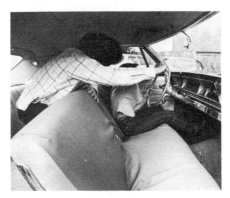

Figure 229

better to wait until one gets into a more advantageous position.

From a sitting or prone position the main counter-attack areas will be the fingers of the weapon hand and then the eyes. If sitting in a car and the attacker approaches from the rear, try to get the hands up before the knife gets all the way to the throat (228), the same as when standing. If you are driving, slam on the brakes and turn the wheels hard, while pulling on the attacker's knife hand (229). This might cause an accident, so be aware of that possibility. At least try to fasten your seat belt before attempting this.

You might, about this time, comment that this doesn't seem like too much. Well, that is true, it isn't too much—precisely because there isn't a whole lot one can do in such a situation. If you think about it, here is a bigger and stronger attacker behind you with a knife at the throat. One can't be in a much worse position. Various martial arts schools and self-defense classes have their favorite techniques to use in such cases. However, this author has never seen any of these techniques work when even a little resistance is put up. Only by moving fast before the knife is actually at the throat and getting the hands up between the knife and throat does one have some chance, even though it is still a risky one. To try to throw, or to elbow in the solar plexus, or stomp on the foot, only gets the throat cut. Do not go on the offensive until the knife is away from the throat, otherwise you are signing your own death warrant. This account does not mean to scare intentionally, only to show that one must have respect for any weapon and think about protec-

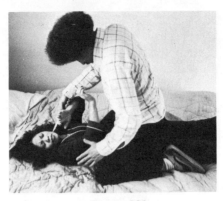

Figure 230

Figure 231

tion first, then attacking afterward.

All the above applies if you are prone also. Get your hand(s) or arm(s) in between you and the knife before it is too late (230) and then strike for the eyes (231).

A woman in one of the author's self-defense classes relates a story. Sleeping face down on her couch wearing only a robe, she awoke to find a man on top of her and a knife at her throat (232). He told her not to move or he would kill her.

Was there anything she could do to stop the rape without risking a sliced throat? Probably not, at least not without using some deception, or doing something disgusting like farting or urinating. In these life-and-death situations where you are at a serious disadvantage, try to use deception or some of the other nonphysical methods of self-defense.

Figure 232

Figure 233

Against Guns

Always remember: against a gun, there is nothing that can be done if the gun is more than a few feet away. You cannot move your body faster than a trigger finger, so you have to attempt subtly to get closer. If that is not possible, don't try anything. Even if the gun is close enough, think twice before trying the techniques below:

Move to the side (233), and hit the gun hand as hard as possible (234), preferably with the palm of the hand. This will deflect the gun long enough to continue the counter-attack and might knock the gun out of the attacker's hand (235). Continue the attack, though; do not get into a wrestling match for the gun, because the stronger person will win. Do not run away,

Figure 234

Figure 235

Figure 236

because no one can outrun a bullet. If possible, kick the gun farther away.

If the gun is against the back of the body or head (236), put

Figure 237

Figure 238

Figure 239

pressure on the gun (237), spin quickly while knocking the gun away with the arm or hand (238), and counter-attack to the head (239).

Obviously, for any weapons practice you can't use the real thing. However, you can use styrofoam bats, rubber knives, and squirt guns. (If you find that your clothes are wet after practicing against a squirt gun, then it is obvious that you were not fast enough.) As against a knife attack, only more so, when confronted by a gun there is no room for a mistake. Mistakes are fatal, so if you do decide to counter-attack, be sure of what to do.

WHAT YOU CAN USE AS A WEAPON

Assuming that you don't want to go out and buy a switch-blade or a gun, there are several things anyone can use as a self-defense weapon. In fact, just about anything can be used as a weapon. However, before attempting to use any of these possible weapons, you must make sure that you learn how to handle them properly. Otherwise the weapon more than likely will be used against you. There are several people who have attempted to ward off an attacker with a weapon, only to have the weapon taken away from them and, in turn, used on them. So if you are going to use a knife, gun, broom handle, mace, or whatever, make sure you know how to use it first.

Various weapons to use include: a purse, knapsack, umbrella, books, boxes, packages, anything being carried, screwdrivers, hammers, wrenches, combs, brushes, hair spray, rings, keys, mace or any type of paralyzing or odiferous sprays, tennis rackets, chairs, glasses, bottles, dishes, records—basically anything that is handy.

HOW TO USE "WEAPONS"

If you are home or at work, there are several things around to throw (the kitchen and the bathroom probably have the most things to throw). Keep up a steady stream of throwing, aim for the head, but don't take very much time to aim. It is better to throw two things and nearly miss than only one thing and nearly miss. If walking outside and you have a purse or knapsack, or are carrying several things, toss them into the attacker's face (240) and kick him in the knee or groin (241) while his attention is distracted. Maybe you will get lucky and seriously hurt him with your throwing implements.

Figure 240

Figure 241

If you are going to use a striking implement such as an umbrella or broom, think of it as a distraction to keep the attacker away. Use it in a jabbing motion and make small circular hits, not big wild swings. Keep the weapon moving constantly; do not let the attacker grab it. If he does grab it, then move in and kick and then strike the head. If using smaller implements such as a hammer, comb, brush, or keys, you will have to be close enough to reach the attacker. Move in and aim for the head. Sensitive areas are the upper lip, lower nose area (242), and windpipe (243) for combs, brushes, and keys—rip them across these areas. Hammers, screwdrivers, or bottles should be used in a circular motion against the head and neck. Use of sprays should be close to the face.

A few things to remember if you are going to use a weapon:

Figure 242

Figure 243

- Keep the weapon handy. Do not keep a weapon at the bottom of the knapsack, purse, or pockets. If walking, keep something to use in the hand. Rummaging at the bottom of the purse or pocket for the "handy" weapon is to give the attacker all the time he needs to knock you out.

- Concentrate on your defense. You still have to protect the body. Several people get cocky when they have a weapon and forget about defending themselves, until after they wake up in the hospital—if they are lucky. The basic defense principles still hold even with weapons. Move out of the way of the attack, block, and then counter.

If using a knife (e.g., in the kitchen), act like the good knife fighter: Be patient, do not try to stab, only slice and nick when the attacker comes near. Do not attack; keep the knife moving in a fast, small, irregular circular and/or figure-eight pattern. Keep the feet fairly close together.

If you have a gun (there are pellet guns and gas guns available that are legal in some states; check with your local police department), keep it handy (with the safety catch on if unattended), either in the hand if outside or within easy reach if at home. Take shooting lessons to learn how to shoot and all the safety criteria. Get a permit, otherwise you might end up in jail for a long time for protecting yourself. Aim for the body when shooting; if off a little bit you might still hit the person. Don't try to aim for an arm or leg; that is much too difficult and only works in the movies. Do not let anyone else play with the gun. Thousands of accidents happen because someone plays with the gun and gets shot "accidentally"; it just isn't worth it. Respect the weapon, whatever it may be, and the odds are that it will be an effective means of self-defense. Treat it carelessly and it won't be effective at all; it will be dangerous to you.

Part 3

Nonphysical Self-Defense Techniques

11

Deception

To be effective, deception has to be subtle. The person being deceived cannot realize that he is being deceived. Some self-defense books and movies show a woman facing an attacker with a gun (244). This woman is a couple of feet away from the attacker and has both hands up in the air. The books or movies explain deception and then show the person wiggling the fingers on one hand or moving one hand slightly (245). Then the attacker is "deceived" into looking at the moving hand and that is when the woman attacks with the other hand or a kick (246). This, of course, works very nicely in the movies and pictures, but, in reality, as soon as the woman moved her hand the attacker would shoot the "deceivor."

To deceive an attacker, you have to get the attacker's mind, if only for a split second, completely off track. In the illustration above a slight hand movement will not do much. That is not to say that a slight hand movement is never able to deceive an attacker, quite the contrary, but you have to learn when and how to use deception. Each self-defense situation is different, and there are no hard and fast rules on how or when to use deception, but there are some general principles and times when it might be necessary.

First of all deception does not have to be physical; it might be as simple as a lie. Tell a would-be rapist that you have venereal disease and carry an old bottle of penicillin pills to "prove" it. Keep a tape recording of a vicious dog barking in the home and play it if you hear any strange sounds. Both of these "tricks" are deceptive and might be enough to stop a possible attack. There are thousands of things as easy to do as this that you can do to protect yourself, and you are limited only by the imagination.

The best time to use physical deception is when you are in easy reach of the attacker with either a strike or a kick. If you are too far away, it takes too much time between the deception and the action. This time gives the attacker a chance to recover, something you don't want. Anything that is being carried or is within easy reach should be used. If a person has packages or a purse, tossing it in the attacker's face and kicking low is a very effective use of deception. **(240, 241).** The attacker only sees the high attack and doesn't see the low kick; after the kick hit high. Or do just the opposite, "accidentally" drop the packages to the ground and look down at them, while striking high; then kick low. In these examples the attacker should be fairly close to the supposed victim, and he should not have a weapon.

As in any type of violent confrontation, when the attack is already in progress, decide what to do, then fake doing something else so that the chances of the real action succeeding are increased. This will usually entail some type of eye movement. In other words look up when attacking low or look down when attacking high. Looking behind someone or calling someone's name at the moment of attack might give an extra edge. Do not deceive and then attack later, there isn't time for that.

If the confrontation is not violent, or at least not violent at that point, you could pretend to go along with it and then react. For example, when a man has had a little too much to drink or is pawing you at a party or some type of social situation, you want to get rid of him but still want to be tactful. Be nice, smile sweetly, slide your hand up slowly and pleasantly to his throat and just press on any of the pressure points while stepping away and saying sorry. Usually he will get the message and leave you alone. If he doesn't, at least you are now away from him and have time to react to any further attack.

When the attacker has a weapon, be patient and wait for a time when you are not so vulnerable, or else don't try anything at all. If the attacker is using a weapon or the confrontation has already become violent, then you will have to apply the above principles. If he is holding a gun or knife on you at a distance and commanding you to do certain things, then do these things until you can get close enough to the attacker to hit the gun hand or arm away. Do not try to kick the hand, as kicks are too

Figure 244

Figure 245

Figure 246

slow, take too much aiming, and the body has to remain stationary while kicking. The object is to get close, hit and move out of the way, then go for a vulnerable area.

As with everything else mentioned in this book, you must always think about protecting yourself. Do not try some type of deceptive movement without being aware of protection, and the consequences of not protecting yourself in case the deceptive act doesn't work. This is always a possibility, no matter what you try. Be aware of this possibility and try to be ready to react in several different ways, whether the situation calls for physical or non-physical responses.

Deception can be very valuable, but like anything else, it must be practiced to be effective. You must have a plan or a reason for using it and move fast and precisely.

12
Situational Responses

Every type of self-defense situation is going to be different. Some might be very violent, some mildly violent, some threateningly violent. Your response should differ accordingly. A street situation is different than a party situation. Weapons can drastically alter the situation. The amount of resistance you employ will vary in any of these situations. A little common sense is also necessary.

If a masher annoys you at a party, for example, a knee in the groin or smash to his nose is not proper retaliation. At the very least you won't be invited back to any more parties. In fact, you will probably go to jail for aggravated assault and battery.

React to the situation. If someone politely approaches, be aware, be polite, and be ready. If your gut reaction is very negative, leave the scene. If you are at a party or any crowded event, a loud "please leave me alone", or "please don't bother me anymore" will usually suffice. There is no reason to get violent unless the other person initiates it.

But, what if you are on the street, alone, and are accosted? Just how much do you resist and what do you do? It is best to think about what you are going to do *right now!* Not when the attack happens, but rather now, when you have the time to think about it and analyze possible alternatives.

After reading this book you should sit down and decide what you will do in various situations so that if you go outside and are accosted you know what to do immediately and react accordingly. You won't have time to think about what to do when a confrontation occurs.

You might be able to talk your way out of the situation or

run away. Perhaps you could stun the attacker with a kick or strike and then get **away**. But, you might have to do more, you might have to **become** very physical and damage the attacker quite **badly**. **Several** comments in this book have been made about **kicking** knees and ripping at the eyes. Probably the eyeballs are the most vulnerable part of the body. Only a little damage here will hurt **the attacker tremendously**. These areas should be used **as a last resort only, not** only because of possible legal ramifications (chapter 16) due to over-reaction, but also because of your own emotional reaction.

The best advice is to be **aware** of where you are, of the potential for violence, of the chances of escape, and of the odds against getting hurt. None of these things are easy to do, especially when you might only have a split second to sum all of this up. But there are no easy answers, and every situation will be different so you will have to be aware of the possibilities. The best way to do this is to start thinking about them now while you have time and not waiting until an actual confrontation.

13

Nonphysical Responses

There are several things that you can do to repulse an attacker without getting into a physical confrontation. Most of the following responses have been used by women to repulse or escape from an attacker. These methods are not guaranteed to work in every situation, but you should certainly be aware of these possibilities.

Talk. It doesn't really matter too much what is said. In fact, several women have not been able to remember what they said during the confrontation. One woman in one of this author's self-defense classes awoke at night to find someone in her bedroom. She got out of bed and kept talking for over an hour before she could manipulate her way over to the window, where she jumped out from the second story. She sprained her ankle badly, but she did get away.

What can you talk about? Anything. Try to talk the person out of the attack. Tell him how bad it will be for him (jail) and for you (pain). Tell him about the police, about how you don't want to get hurt, about how someone is expecting you shortly— anything to keep him away. You will probably end up repeating yourself several times, but that is all right as long as it is working.

Run. If you can, run—and yell as you run. (Don't scream. A yell is a loud controlled voice; a scream is a panic-stricken voice, and people are more apt to turn away from screaming.) It is best to yell "fire" or something else to get people's attention. If you have on high heels, you won't be able to run away, at least not without taking the shoes off. Whatever you do, don't trip and fall, and don't keep looking back to see if the attacker is gaining. Every time you turn around slows you down, and you want to run as fast as possible. If the attacker is close, you will be able to hear his footsteps and heavy breathing, so you don't have to turn around. If he is gaining on you and you aren't close to safety, stop, turn, move to the side quickly, kick the legs or strike for the head, then take off running again. If you are lucky, you will connect somewhere and give yourself additional time to get to safety.

Fainting. Fainting or pretending to faint might work (even though this author does not recommend it) especially if someone grabs you, because now they have to hold you up and that takes energy. If you do pretend to faint and the attacker doesn't leave, you will have to wait until he gets close enough and then lash out with all of your energy to surprise and hurt him. Then get away as fast as possible. There are some serious drawbacks to this particular means of self-defense, one being that you will usually fall to the ground and, as mentioned before, it is better to be on your feet throughout any confrontation. But the main drawback is that if your "surprise" attack doesn't work, then you are much more vulnerable.

Act "crazy." Usually, an attacker thinks he is dealing with a "normal" person; if you can convince him that you aren't normal, he might leave. Women have done such things as getting down on all fours, eating grass and making sounds like a cow, or hopping up and down on one leg, flapping the arms and making airplane sounds. Some start giggling and making funny faces. One of my woman friends said that she was hassled by a guy and that she started making faces and drooling at the mouth. That was enough to turn off the attacker and force him to leave. Try anything that you think is crazy. At the worst, it could postpone the assault, give you more time to think; at best it might cause the attacker to leave.

Act in an unexpected manner. Become very domineering or very motherly or sisterly. One woman who worked at a counseling center demanded that the attacker make an appointment with the psychiatrist to straighten out his problem, gave him the psychiatrist's card, and walked away leaving the would-be attacker literally flabbergasted. Others have tried to help the attacker, offering advice and counseling. One woman pulled out a Bible and started reading from it, offering to help the attacker find Jesus and mend his evil ways.

Insult the attacker, especially sexually. Assuming the attack is sexual, you might become sexually aggressive, try to hurry the guy on, or you can say something like you hope he lasts longer than two seconds, or comment on the size of his penis: compare it to a flea. This is especially good against sexual assaults, because obviously the attacker has sexual problems and ego problems. Recent research out of New England has indicated that fifty percent of rapes end with the attacker ejaculating before penetration. So some disparaging comment about his performance could make him forget the whole attempt.

Turn off the attacker. Actions designed to make the attacker want to get away immediately, such as slobbering over yourself, blowing your nose without using a tissue, sticking your finger up your nose or in your ears, urinating, farting, defecating, vomiting, or anything else you can think of that is repulsive or disgusting, can be used as methods to repulse the attacker.

All of these methods have been used successfully by women to ward off attackers. Although this doesn't guarantee that any of them will be successful for you, at least you can add them to the list of possible ways of resisting. But, always be ready for an actual physical confrontation.

14

Avoiding Confrontations

has been assumed that you have ... ...e to react in some manner, be it ... ...physi... ...there are several ways to avoid ... ... Most ... ...un are common sense and you know ... ... but they will be repeated here for your convenience. There are other things you can do that you might not be aware ... ... here ... ...t of. These particular things are des... ... ...attack... ...just to make it much harder for the ... ... to succe... ...you have to do are a few simple thi... ...think about ... ...festyle, living conditions, and see wha... ... ...one to ... ... them from a safety standpoint. ... ...few minutes ... y for about a week is all you will hav... ...on some ... ...se things, and then you can forget ... ... Other... ...will have to try to make a habit of ... ...they become ... ...nd nature as brushing your teeth or combing your hair. A little effort on your part will go a long way in thwarting possible attacks.

10 WAYS TO MAKE YOUR HOME SAFER

Approximately 40 to 50 percent of all atta... ... ... in the home which is not quite as far as possible ... ...but here you should have the advantage of knowing the layout of the house or apartment. Knowing the location of ... ... doors, light switches, objects in use as weapons, and the floor "creaks" may save your life.

How can you make your home safer?

1. Lock all the windows and doors every ... ... and when you are ...

2. Install a peephole so you can see who ... ...

the door.

3. Install deadbolt locks; they are inconvenient but much safer than ordinary locks. Also get the kind of sliding locks that bolt into the wall.

4. Put blocks on your windows so they can only open so far.

5. Keep your phone number unlisted, or if you do list it, do not include the address in the listing. Use only your first initial and last name, or add a male name with yours, such as "John and Mary Smith . . . 268-1111." (Even if there isn't a John, a would-be attacker doesn't know that.) In many cases, the sexual assaulter stakes out the intended victim. Living alone makes you a likely candidate for attack.

6. Put only your last name on the mailbox, or, again, add a male name to it even if you live alone. The attacker can't be sure you will be alone.

7. Don't advertise that you are alone. Keep shades or drapes drawn. When you know you are coming home after dark, turn on the porch light and leave on an inside light, or use timer switches to conserve electricity.

8. Don't open the door to strangers; if they want to use a phone, tell them that you will call for them. Bonified sales people, repair persons, and officers of the law carry proper identification, and if you still have doubts, call the number on their identification to check.

9. Get to know your neighbors. This is more and more difficult to do with our transient and slightly paranoid society, but it is an excellent security precaution. If neighbors see anything unusual, they can help you, and in turn, you can help them, even if it means nothing more than a simple phone call.

10. Obscene phone calls should be dealt with by hanging up immediately. If they are repeated, report them to the phone company and get a new phone number. You can also keep a loud whistle by the phone and blow it into the receiver when the person calls. Insults can work sometimes. A good woman friend of mine told me of her effective means of stopping obscene phone calls. She kept getting sexual obscene phone calls for over a week, from the same person. Finally she said, quite calmly, to the caller, "You know, I'll bet your penis is the size of a gnat." With that came stunned silence from the other end,

and then a dial tone. They never called back. The author has no statistics on the subject but several of his students have noted that they received obscene phone calls immediately before an attack. Since it has been documented that an intended victim has usually been staked out by the attacker it is not hard to follow that the attacker could use obscene phone calls as a means of intimidation.

CAR AND TRAVEL SAFETY

- Lock your car when away from it, but be aware that most street kids can jimmy a lock in about two seconds.
- Look in the back seat before getting in, lock the doors after getting in. Keep windows closed in the back and on the front passenger side, or open them only partially if it is a hot day.
- Try to park in well-lit and well-traveled areas. Paying at a protected parking lot might be worth the money.
- When going to the car, have the keys out and ready; don't fumble around in the purse or pockets for the keys. This is also a good practice for going to your house or office.
- If you are followed by another car, drive to the nearest police station, fire station, or hospital emergency room. Even any open store or gas station is okay. *Don't drive home or to a friend's home.* If absolutely necessary, speed, honk the horn, flash your lights—anything to draw the police.
- If you are hitchhiking, take rides only from women, older people, or couples, though this is more difficult to do because they usually won't pick up hitchhikers. Notice the license number as you approach the car and find out where the driver is going first. If the driver offers to take you wherever you want, be very wary. The same holds true for two or more males in a car, especially if you can smell alcohol or see empty beer cans or bottles in the car.

If the driver makes a wrong turn or starts going in the wrong direction, try to get out the instant that the car stops or even slows down. If you can't get out, roll down the window and yell for help or throw things out the window to draw attention to the car. Inform the driver that you have his license number and don't believe any story about shortcuts. If none of these tactics work, bring your legs up, turn toward him and bracing your back against the door, start kicking at him. He will have to worry about not wrecking the car and will be getting hurt at the same time. Be careful and prepare yourself for a possible crash. This is dangerous, but it might be better than the other possibilities. If he stops the car, open the door, get out, and run away as fast as possible.

OUTSIDE ENVIRONMENT

When outside, stay by well-lighted areas as much as possible; in other words, don't walk down dark alleys at night. Vary your route when walking (or driving also) home, to the stores, or wherever. Try to walk with someone whenever you can, and walk in busy areas. If you notice someone following you, go to the nearest store, house, police station, or wherever it is fairly safe. You can walk down the middle of the street if the sidewalks are dark and deserted, but watch out for the drivers. If approached, yell "fire" and you'll probably get more results and help than if you yelled "help" or "rape."

Keep your head up and look like you know where you are going. Walk quickly and somewhat aggressively. Most people that look vulnerable, shy, and easily intimidated walk slower and keep their head down. Do just the opposite and you will cause most attackers to go look elsewhere for a more docile victim.

If you are in a building, learn the location of emergency exits, doors that you can lock, and phones. Check elevators before getting in and, if someone looks suspicious near the elevator or your office door, turn around and go in the opposite direction. Don't get in an elevator with anyone you don't trust or feel wrong about.

15

A Different Kind of Rape

"I'm riding in your car
You turn on the radio
You draw me close. I just say no
I say I don't like it
But, you know I'm a liar
Cause when you kiss, ooh, ooh, fire." [1]

This hit single "Fire" by the Pointer Sisters raises some very serious questions about communication between the sexes. As pointed out in previous chapters, no woman wants to be raped. But, do women want to be seduced? And if they do, where is the line drawn between seduction, and forceful seduction?

A few years ago these kinds of questions weren't thought about too much. Lately, a different kind of rape has been identified. It goes by various names, but basically it is an "acquaintance" rape. It could be a very casual encounter with a close friend, even with a husband. The courts are beginning to take notice of this new definition also.

A discussion of these points and questions usually leads to more points and questions, but they should be dealt with. The reader should know what to do, and how to react in certain situations, and as this book has pointed out on several occasions, it is important to think about these things now. Not when the situation occurs. First of all it must be understood that no woman wants to be raped. Rape is not a sexual experience. It is a domination of one person over another. It is a power trip. Sex is the instrument through which this dominance takes place. Anyone who thinks that rape is not that big a deal is entirely

[1] The song "Fire" is from the Pointer Sisters album "Energy," on the Planet label by Electra, Asylum Nonesuch.

wrong. It is an extremely emotional and terrible experience.

But, what about seduction? It might seem easy to determine the differences between seduction and rape, but is it really that easy? In a sexually permissive society a lot of men come to expect sex from any and every woman that they go out with. Men think that if they spend money on a female then the female should come through. Sometimes it is hard for a man to know where to draw the line.

Probably 99.9% of all men have been told at one time or another that a woman doesn't mean no when she says no. And, a lot of times women don't mean no when they say no. They might feel that they have to say no because it is the proper thing to do. This only confuses the situation more, for both sexes.

Let's examine a situation where two people meet, are mutually attracted, go out once and are feeling pretty good. They go back to his or her place and he wants to have sex. She says no, but he "knows" what "no" really means. He continues his seductive efforts. She likes him, but doesn't want to have sex. Where does she draw the line? How does she let him know where the line is? Can he tell where the line is? Will he stop? These are difficult questions to answer and will vary in practically every situation. To make it even harder to answer these questions, let's assume this couple has known each other for a while and has gone out together several times.

If the seductive efforts continue, is there a point in time where it can lead to rape? Most definitely yes. If the female really doesn't want to have sex with the male and tells him so repeatedly, and the male continues, and gets frustrated at her "lack of understanding" then there is a possibility that the situation could turn violent, even with a supposedly normal male.

What if the woman only wants to go so far? Perhaps just some hugging, kissing, or even gentle caressing, but nothing more. It is difficult to tell a male friend or aquaintance that it is OK to do this, this and this, but not that or that!

The situation becomes almost ridiculous. A male wants to have sex with a woman who, as far as he knows, wants to have sex, even if she says no. The more they see each other and the more intimate they become over a period of time (this could be one night, several days, or months) the more he wants it and the more he thinks she wants it. What can the woman do in this situation, especially if she is not entirely sure of her feelings?

It is a very simple answer, but probably one of the hardest things to do in the world. COMMUNICATE. If necessary communicate firmly. By communicating the woman takes control of the situation. The man no longer controls everything. You tell him what you want or expect, or don't want. This way he understands, or should understand, exactly what is expected of him and you have put yourself in control.

Make it clear that yes you would like to have a nite cap or see his house or show your apartment, but that is all. As the relationship progresses (once again over a period of time from hours to years) you can change your expectations if you want, and let him know.

What if the woman is not sure of what she wants? The suggestion is to be conservative at first. Go slowly. If the male isn't interested, then you haven't lost much. If he is, he will be back. Besides, you can always change your mind. But as long as you know what you are doing and where you are going you can control what is happening. This is the best way to keep the "acquaintance" rape or forcible seduction out of your life.

16
Emotional Aspects

WHOSE FAULT IS IT ANYHOW?

Continuing the scene from the last chapter, imagine that a woman and a man are together in the woman's apartment. They are sitting, talking and he starts his seductive efforts. She says no—he persists. Pretty soon he is out of control and she doesn't or can't resist. The woman might think that it is her fault. She feels she has been raped, but she is not sure. After all she did let him in the apartment and maybe she liked him somewhat. Perhaps her outfit was too sexy. Maybe it was her fault. Was it rape? And is she equally to blame?

Was it rape? Yes. Anytime a woman says no and means it and has made it clear to the man and he persists, then yes it is rape. Whether the scene was physically violent or not the man has dominated the woman and sex was used as the means to achieve this dominance.

Is she equally to blame? No. Once again, as long as she has made it clear what she wants and if her wants are denied by force then she cannot be blamed for the situation getting out of control. If she has led the man on, teased him, indicated that sex was a possibility, then perhaps she should take some blame. But this is more of a problem of communication. If the woman is forceful in communicating what she wants and lets the man know it right from the start, then the problem of rape shouldn't occur. If it still does then she cannot have any blame.

GUILT

Will the woman feel guilty? Probably. Looking back on any rape situation there are probably things that the woman realizes she could have done differently to avoid the situation. The aquaintance male in the woman's apartment could have been handled differently. Afterwards she thinks that perhaps she shouldn't have offered a drink, or taken off her shoes, or done a million other things that one does not even think about, until afterwards.

There are other situations. When outdoors try to be aware of all the events that are going on around you. Avoid potential harmful situations. Sometimes situations don't look harmful. A stranger asks for directions and then pulls you into a car or the bushes because you got too close to him. If indoors check your dwelling. Millions of women have been raped in their own beds because someone came in through an unlocked door or window. A woman could feel guilty and stupid about these different situations. If she realizes that she was not totally in control of the situation when she could have been, or at least more in control, then she will have a tendency to blame herself and feel guilty.

The guilt can be used positively however, and this is what any woman who has been raped or attacked should do. Look at the situation and try to analyze it. Counselors or women's centers can be of great help here. Find out why the attack happened and analyze what could have been done to prevent it.

In the aquaintance rape situation, what could have been done? Communication, tell the person what is expected of him. Don't be so cozy, etc. etc. When outdoors don't get close to anyone you don't know and trust. Indoors, double check all locks. Simple things like these can make you more aware of yourself and your surroundings. This in turn lets you be in control of yourself and your surroundings. When you can do this you have made a big step in the right direction to avoiding a rape situation. Avoidance is the key to leading a safe life.

AFTER AN ATTACK

If you are assaulted in any way, the effects emotionally can be very traumatic. How traumatic or how much it will affect each individual can cover a whole range of responses. Friends, family, and counseling can play a large role in helping the individual recover and get back to leading a regular life. Whatever the situation, the victim should realize that the attack was not her fault; no one asks to be attacked. The victim will recover; there might be physical pain or scars on top of the mental and emotional pain, but, with time, one will recover. How much time is dependent upon the woman and the help received from friends.

The first thing an assault victim should attempt to do is regain the control over her own life. Getting back in the normal routine is very important to a fast recovery.

There is always some type of professional counseling in the area. Larger metropolitan areas usually have several specifically oriented counseling centers for the assault victim. There are psychiatrists, clergy, hospital staff, and other professional help available no matter where you live.

Family and friends are probably the most important factor in helping the victim recover from an attack. Their understanding and help are very important. This is especially true of husbands and steady male friends. It might even be advisable for the husband or friends to go to the counseling sessions also. Unfortunately, a statistic that most people are not aware of indicates that up to 50 percent of relationships with the spouse or steady male friend disintegrates within a year's time after a sexual assault. This indicates that most men still have a long way to go before understanding the rape victim.

A sexual assault is never enjoyable, and it is not easily preventable, especially when the attacker is bigger and stronger than the victim. No one asks to be attacked. Unfortunately, it might take several more decades before enough men, and some women also, realize this. Hopefully, with time, this will change. Laws are just beginning to change, so that it is the attacker and not the victim who is put on trial. Attitudes change more slowly, but they do change.

This author has asked men with this archaic attitude if they would like to be raped. Of course, they say no and add that no one could rape them. The author then tells them that if he was so inclined, he could rape them. The looks on their faces are quite enlightening. Most of them know of his martial arts training, and, even though he is not a big bruiser type, many of these men are instantly aware of the possibility of being a victim. The author feels that if these men think about it, they come out of the conversation with a more realistic idea about what that type of confrontation could be like.

Counseling and talking with professionals, friends, and family, and a general understanding of what an encounter does to a person can help everyone involved. It is even a good idea to discuss with friends and family about your and their reaction to an assault. With this understanding, it will be much easier to get back to the normal routine.

17
Legal Concerns

Legal aspects cover two basic areas. One is how far you can go in defending yourself, and the other is what you can do to help put the attacker behind bars.

Several self-defense classes and books (this one no exception) include some pretty gory and deadly techniques. What happens if you use these on the street for self-defense? Are you likely to go to jail for protecting yourself? The answer is no—with some important qualifications.

1. For these physical self-defense tactics to be legally justifiable, the attacker must initiate some type of physical confrontation. If someone whistles at you or says "Hi, baby," or even something derogatory, it is best to just ignore it and continue on your way. Kicking someone or scratching their eyes out is too drastic for that situation. In a physical confrontation where the attacker makes a move toward you, you should defend yourself to the utmost and try to get away. If the attacker falls and is hurt, leave fast; don't kick him or any other such tactic.

2. If the attacker uses a weapon, it usually means you will have to use more deadly or painful tactics to protect yourself, and this is quite justified with the same provisions as above.

3. If you do carry a weapon, such as a knife or a gun (properly registered), you can't use it without proper judgment. You cannot go around shooting or stabbing people indiscriminately just because you think something worse might happen. However, if someone is in your home and is trying to attack you, and you use a bottle, knife, or even a gun, the situation is different and you have the right to use these instruments to protect yourself.

4. Check with your local police about what you can do. Every state differs in its laws. Some are very progressive, others not so progressive. The laws are also being changed and revised constantly. This is especially true concerning women's rights to self-protection. Your best bet is to call the police station and find out exactly what the law says, or consult a lawyer.

A few states have found that it is hard to prosecute a rape case and even if a person is prosecuted and convicted the penalties are minor in comparison to the crime. What some states have done (and this is usually true only if the rape or attack occurs in the home) is to charge the attacker with several crimes such as burglary, breaking and entering, aggravated assault, etc.

Burglary is defined (the following is paraphrased for simplicity) as entering a home with the intent to commit a theft or felony. Rape is a felony. California law states that burglary in the first degree is punishable by not less than five years in prison. Rape is punishable by not less than three years in prison. (It should be noted that judges use the penal code as a guide and the actual sentences can vary quite a bit.) Burglary in the first degree carries a stiffer sentence than does rape. Burglary is also much easier to prove. If someone has entered your home with the intent to rape you, then he can be charged with attempted rape and burglary, even if he doesn't rape you. He only has to have the intent to do it. Intent can be somewhat difficult to prove at times, but the burglary charge can still stand.

What does this mean to you as the intended victim?

1. If you are raped in your home and the rapist escapes, make sure that the charges filed against him include burglary. If you have to, tell the police that he stole something, like money or jewelry.

2. If a rape is attempted in your home and the rapist escapes, do exactly the same as in number 1. The police will look for a person accused of two or three charges more than they will for just a petty theft or just a rape attempt. The judges are also stricter with sentencing with two or three charges than just one charge.

3. If you are confronted in your home and you have a gun or

knife and wound or even kill the attacker, there will be a very thorough investigation. You should do everything possible, in the eyes of the law, to put yourself in a favorable position and the attacker in the worst possible position. While you might think that it is a straightforward self-defense case, the law and all of the quirks that go with it don't necessarily think the same. A retired police officer acquaintance of the author's stated that in a case such as the one described above where the attacker has been killed, he would advise the woman to get a kitchen knife and put it in the attacker's hand and put some of her money or a wallet in his pocket and then call the police.

While this book will not attempt to get into moral issues over this type of advice it certainly does advocate doing everything possible to get rapists off the street and into prison.

The second aspect of legal concern is how to put the attacker behind bars. First, it is recommended that you report the crime, and report it *immediately.* The longer you wait to report it, the longer the attacker has to make his escape. The faster the report, the greater the chances of capture. If the attack is not reported, for whatever reason, the attacker is reassured of his expertise and will continue his attacks. If he is fearful of getting caught, this might slow him down or stop his attempts altogether. A good description of the attacker will make him more wary and easier to catch.

If you are attacked, call the police and go to the hospital or a doctor. Do not go home, wash up, change clothes, and then call the police or the hospital. You have just destroyed the evidence, and there is still enough skepticism and chauvinism in police departments and on hospital staffs to not trust your account. The actual exam might not be pleasant, but it is necessary to make the legal system work in its own way.

If a suspect is arrested and you have to go to court, be prepared for an emotional experience. The defendant's lawyer will more than likely try to do everything possible to discredit your testimony. Fortunately, in some states the laws are changing so that your previous sex life or lifestyle will not be admitted as testimony, but that is true in only some states.

You should not worry about a further attack from the same

person, either after the trial or after he gets out of jail, if he goes. This type of thing does happen occasionally, but usually it is closer to movie plot than reality. The attacker realizes that he will be watched more carefully and be more suspect if he is accused or convicted, and most do not want to have anything to do with you ever again.

The legal aspects of reporting an attack and going all the way through court procedures can be a time-consuming and an emotionally draining experience. But it is necessary in order to get rapists and assaulters off the streets and keep them off.